WIN THE JOB INTERVIEW BEFORE IT BEGINS

THE
FIRST
6
SECONDS

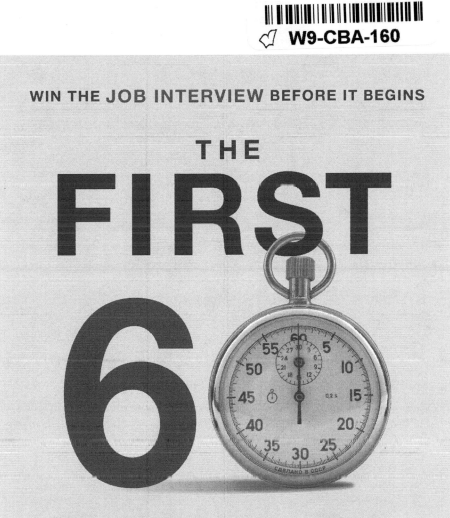

DAN BURNS

 SOURCEBOOKS, INC.®
NAPERVILLE, ILLINOIS

Published by Sourcebooks, Inc.
P.O. Box 4410, Naperville, Illinois 60567-4410
(630) 961-3900
Fax: (630) 961-2168
www.sourcebooks.com

Library of Congress Cataloging-in-Publication Data

Burns, Dan.
  The first 60 seconds : win the job interview before it begins / Dan Burns.
      p. cm.
  Includes bibliographical references and index.
  1. Employment interviewing. I. Title. II. Title: First 60 seconds.
  HF5549.5.I6B87 2009
  650.14′4--dc22

                          2008051385

Printed and bound in the United States of America
POD 10 9 8 7 6 5 4 3

To Lori, Katie, and David

Acknowledgments

I would like to thank the following people, without whom this book would never have become a reality:

- My editor, Peter Lynch, and all of the great people at Sourcebooks. Thank you for your belief in the idea and the conviction to see that idea develop into this great book.

- All of the mentors whom I have been privileged to work with and learn from. I will forever cherish our relationship and know that your wisdom and guidance continues to influence me in everything I do.

- Everyone whose path I crossed in all of my business endeavors, specifically those who gave a young man a chance when no one else would, with particular regard to my good friends in Chicago and Dallas.

- My friends, family, and two beautiful children, for their continual and unconditional love and support. You are all the best!

- My father and mother, Leonard and Anita Burns, who provided a supportive and nurturing environment and who instilled in me the value of hard work, the importance of family, and the belief that anything is possible.

- Most importantly, my wife Lorraine, my better half and best friend, who not only does everything possible to bring strength and stability to our family but also stands by me and with me down whatever path lies ahead. You are the best.

Contents

Introduction: It All Happens in 60 Seconds vii

Section 1: The 60-Day Plan

Chapter 1: Overview of the 60-Day Plan 3

Chapter 2: Assessing and Understanding Your Job
　　　　　and Career Market 8

Chapter 3: The Company Profile 18

Chapter 4: The Job Profile 23

Chapter 5: Your Personal Profile 28

Chapter 6: Your Professional Experience Inventory 36

Chapter 7: Preparing Your Credentials 43

Chapter 8: Presenting Your Credentials 60

Chapter 9: Arranging the Job Interview 71

Chapter 10: Honing Your Communication Skills 81

Chapter 11: Preparing for the Interview 89

Chapter 12: Dressing Up Your Image 98

Section 2: The First 60 Seconds

Chapter 13: What You Can Accomplish in 60 Seconds 109

Chapter 14: The Final Countdown 111

Chapter 15: The First Look 119

Chapter 16: The Greeting 125

Chapter 17: The Relationship 129

Chapter 18: *The First 60 Seconds:* Final Thoughts
　　　　　and Considerations 136

Section 3: Managing the Next 60 Minutes

Chapter 19: Setting the Stage for the Interview 145

Chapter 20: Summarize Your Qualifications 155

Chapter 21: Continue Developing a Relationship with
the Interviewer 166

Chapter 22: Understand What's in It for You 172

Chapter 23: I'm Available! What's Next? 179

Section 4: The Close

Chapter 24: Post-Interview Communications 187

Chapter 25: The Offer Letter and Employment Agreement 201

Chapter 26: Your First Day 219

Section 5: Your 60-Month Career Plan

Chapter 27: The Future Begins Now 227

Chapter 28: Goals and Plans 234

Chapter 29: Prospecting for Career Growth
and Opportunity 246

Chapter 30: Preparing Yourself for Your Next
Career Opportunity 258

Chapter 31: *The First 60 Seconds* for Life 262

Epilogue : *The First 60 Seconds* for Life 267

List of Exhibits 270

Index 272

About the Author 276

It All Happens in 60 Seconds

A hiring manager makes a decisive qualification of a job candidate within the first 60 seconds of the time they meet.

That's it. You have 60 seconds to make the sale of your product and service *(you)* and close the deal on your next career opportunity. Are you ready?

Over the last fifteen years, I have used and developed my skills as a hiring manager in a variety of business disciplines. Additionally, as an owner and manager of a successful IT management and consulting firm, I had the opportunity to work closely with hiring managers to help them make their employment and hiring methods more successful. Our firm had been successful in helping clients hire more than one thousand employees and consultants. I wish I could say that those one thousand hires were the result of an identical number of candidate job interviews, but unfortunately that was not the case. A successful hire was sometimes the result of two or more individual and different candidate interviews. As a result, our company was involved in coordinating and overseeing more than fifteen-hundred interviews over a fifteen-year period.

It is becoming increasingly difficult to hire employees in an effective and efficient manner. It is simply more difficult to find the best-qualified job candidate from a growing universe of available candidates. Job seekers share a similar concern in that they feel it is increasingly difficult to compete for opportunities.

The Job Seeker Has Taken the Job Interview Process for Granted

For any hiring employer, the process of identifying, selecting, and hiring a new employee is as challenging as ever. More time, resources, and budget dollars are allocated to the task, and the tools and options available for identifying and hiring new resources continue to proliferate. Employers always look for the best possible prospective employee among a field of candidates that in many cases is so extensive and diverse that managing the process effectively has become quite difficult. Hiring managers are charged with filling open positions in the most timely and cost-effective way possible, while at the same time following the rules and guidelines of the HR department and company management.

For most job seekers, there are three primary activities in the job search process. The first activity focuses on the identification of new job opportunities. Second is the submission of a résumé or credentials. The third activity focuses on the job interview itself. We typically spend a great deal of time and effort on the first two activities right away, identifying and narrowing the field of opportunities and then submitting résumés. What usually follows is a substantial and frustrating waiting period.

When an individual receives a response from an interested potential employer, the focus shifts to the interview. Typically the interview lasts an hour, and the candidate expects that hour to be sufficient for the hiring manager to find out or obtain everything necessary to select a candidate for the position.

Our fast-paced lifestyle supports this assumption. While trying to manage a career and pursue new and exciting opportunities, the employee is still required to work a full day. Add to that the challenges of our personal lives—whether we're striving to be a responsible and involved parent, visit the gym, or play as a weekend musician—and there's not enough time in the day to focus on our career future. If an individual is out of work, between jobs, or looking for that first career opportunity, the added stress makes the situation even worse.

The result is troubling. When you pursue new career opportunities, you try to get your name out there, submit résumés to a few job openings, then wait for the call. When you don't get the job, you're disappointed, and you wait, frustrated, until the next call comes.

This is not the way it should be. We think that if we submit a résumé and get the interview, there's a good chance we'll get the job. Most of us don't think about it, but much more should be done—and it doesn't require an excessive amount of additional time or effort.

If you want to be successful in reaching that next stage of your career, you need to respect the hiring process and do everything within your power to navigate through that process in an effective and efficient manner. You need to focus not only on the job interview, but also on everything before and after the interview to ensure your success in the process. You cannot take the interview process for granted.

It's Extremely Difficult to Differentiate

When you submit credentials for a position, you're not the only one interested in the job. Likely you are one of dozens or maybe even hundreds of candidates interested in the position. If you're fortunate enough to get an interview, you're only one in a field of candidates being interviewed.

Sure, you try to prepare a complete, concise, and professional résumé. Maybe you'll even prepare a cover letter or introductory email to go along with the résumé. The credentials go out in the mail or are submitted via an employer's online submission tool, and you're done. That you ever hear back on a submission is an amazing occurrence, given the unknown path that the credentials take. You show up for the interview and hope you have the opportunity and ability to set yourself apart from the other candidates being considered.

Following this typical approach, you are most likely doing the same thing as everyone else, and for the hiring manager, it can be impossible to differentiate one résumé from the next. Getting selected for a job in this manner is, at best, a chance happening.

It doesn't have to be that way.

Get the Job before the Interview Even Takes Place!

The first 60 seconds of your meeting with a prospective employer are important, but you don't really want the success of your job interview to hinge on a quick 60 seconds. It's important to look at the job interview as just one part of a longer-term, larger scope, and multi-faceted process.

Everything you do in the 60 days prior to the interview will determine your interviewing success. Most of your competition will simply show up for their interviews and attempt to talk about their résumés and qualifications. For you, the interview can be the final formality in an extensive process to win over your new boss.

The First 60 Seconds gives an easy, step-by-step approach addressing the many potential variables of the hiring process. You can choose to focus on each of the strategies, or you can supplement your career plan with ideas you find here. Most of all, you will be making a positive, proactive effort to manage the job interview process, your career, and your future success.

Be Proactive and Not Reactive

The majority of the time, you think about making a career change as a reaction to some event in your life. Maybe your current job is not quite working out as you had planned. Or maybe your expenses have increased, and your salary isn't covering them they way it used to. Or you've encountered one of those life events (marriage, first child, caring for elderly parents) that trigger you to think about your career, where you're headed, and the next steps you should take. Regardless of the triggering event, you're confronted with a situation where you must react, and only because of that event did you even consider your career situation.

When you have to react in this way, you put unnecessary boundaries on how you might address the situation. Planning is impaired, time frames are set, and immediate change is desired. The greatest impact of a reactive action is on timing. When you react, you consciously or unconsciously place a time parameter on achieving a desired change or resolution. When you limit the time to address your career planning and career changes, you end up doing only those things that can be done within your pre-defined time frame.

In *The First 60 Seconds*, you'll learn a series of activities that will help you manage your career in a more proactive manner. No more scrambling the night before the interview trying to prepare something intelligent to say. No more rash job changes, making a move because you have to. No more sitting idly by while others step in front of you (and on top of you) in your quest for new and exciting job opportunities.

After today, you will proactively manage your career. By doing so, you will understand your overall career plan and where you are with respect to that plan. You'll know where you're going, how you'll get there, and how far you have traveled on your journey to success. You will have all the tools necessary to effectively manage each and every aspect of the job search and job change process, enhanced by the ability to differentiate yourself from the crowd.

Dare to Be Different

Attempting to secure your next career opportunity can be extremely challenging in today's competitive market. There are a lot of smart and talented people in the world, and you will be up against some of them as you interview for your next job. When it comes time for the hiring manager to select the best candidate for the job, what will he or she take into consideration, beyond the résumé, cover letter, and standard interview questions? The hiring manager will look for qualities that make a candidate shine and stand out. All you have to do is make the effort to show the hiring manager how you stand apart.

Throughout this book, you will notice that we will focus quite a bit on differentiation. Differentiation is not about being eccentric or unusual. In job-search terms, it means rising to a level above the norm. With a small amount of extra effort, you will be able to differentiate yourself from those who are standing in the way of your future career success.

The differentiator icon will help you quickly spot the major differentiators in *The First 60 Seconds* approach.

All you need is the willingness to make the additional effort, and you'll manage your career on your terms, according to your plan. Essentially, you'll make the additional effort to take control of your life.

Let's get started!

Maxims of *The First 60 Seconds* Approach

- On a job interview, in a business setting, and in every encounter you have with another person, **the other person will make a decisive qualification of you within the first 60 seconds of the time you meet.** Expect it, prepare for it, and make the best of it.

- In attempting to get that next great career opportunity, while important, **your résumé is not the key to your success;** everything else you can do is what differentiates you from the rest and gives you the edge.

- In attempting to get that next great career opportunity, while important, **the interview is not the key to your success;** everything you do in the first 60 seconds of meeting your prospective employer, everything you can do in the 60 days prior to the interview, and every step you take after the interview will determine your success.

- Beating out the competition is all about **differentiation**—setting yourself apart from the masses and showing your unique strengths and qualities. The simple key to differentiation is making a focused and concerted effort to **surpass what is normally expected**.

- **Proactive management** of your job search process *and* your long-term career plan is the key to achieving the career and financial success you deserve.

- The success of your *First 60 Seconds* encounter is dependent upon **everything you do prior** to that encounter and **everything you do after** that encounter as you manage your long-term goals and plans.

- Career growth and personal development **is achievable** through **small, continuous, and incremental change** that can be sustained over a long period of time.

Are you ready?

Section 1

The 60-Day Plan

Make no little plans; they have no magic to stir men's blood.
—*Daniel Hudson Burnham*

We never know how high we are
Till we are called to rise
And then, if we are true to plan
Our statures touch the skies.
—*Emily Dickinson*

CHAPTER 1

Overview of the 60-Day Plan

I Need a New Job or a Career Change Now! Why 60 Days?

The whole point of the 60-day or two-month period is to focus on the bigger picture of what the job change process is all about. Some candidates obsess over the interview. While the interview does play a part, the job change process is really about doing more than your competition and differentiating you from all other job candidates. It's about developing a proactive plan for pursuing the interview process. It's about making a great first impression with a hiring manager before you even have a chance to meet. It's about spending an appropriate and manageable amount of time on one of the most important activities of your life—getting that next new and exciting job as you climb your career ladder.

There are dozens of variables and criteria that go into a hiring manager's decision, including a candidate's prior and relevant experience, résumé format and presentation, first impression, interpersonal skills, image, personality, professionalism, work ethic, career aspirations, etc. It is extremely important that you try to manage as many variables as possible. The more variables you manage effectively, the greater your chance for being selected for the position. The fewer you manage, the greater the risk that you will be negatively impacted.

Consider a situation where a hiring manager's decision-making process consists of only two variables:

1. Does the candidate's résumé reflect the type of experience I'm looking for?

2. Did the candidate meet our skill expectations based on the test he or she took at the interview?

There are only two variables, each equally weighed to make the decision. What happens if your résumé format is not exactly what the interviewer is looking for or doesn't adequately convey your experience? You have lost half of your chance. What if you're not a good test taker, or on that particular day you're not as focused as you usually are, or you didn't happen to prepare for three of the five questions that were asked? There goes the other half.

On the other hand, what if there are ten variables, each equally weighed? If you miss out on one variable, you still have the ability to meet expectations on 90 percent of the other variables. By following the strategies in this book, you will create so many other variables and will impress the interviewer on so many other fronts that you will still get the job.

Since different hiring managers look for different things, there are dozens of variables that can go into the decision-making process. Many variables may not necessarily be at the top of the interviewer's list—but they can be if you put them there. You can add variables to the interviewer's list that he or she may never have considered.

In this section, we will cover the most important things to consider as you plan out your approach to securing a job. After the 60-Day Plan has been executed, we will proceed to the next stage (hopefully just a formality) of the interviewing process. We'll cover in detail the first 60 seconds of your meeting with the interviewer, how to manage the first 60 minutes of the interview itself, what you need to do to close the deal, and how to put the finishing touches on your decision to accept that new position.

It is important that your 60-Day Plan be part of a larger, overall career plan. In the last section of this book, you'll develop a 60-Month Plan with detailed and achievable one- and five-year goals. With this broad plan, executable short-term strategies, and a proven 60-day job acquisition approach, you will have everything you need to proactively and effectively manage the rest of your career. Exhibit 1.1 shows the 60-Day Plan and how it fits into a larger career management approach that we cover throughout this book.

Exhibit 1.1
The First 60 Seconds Career Management Approach

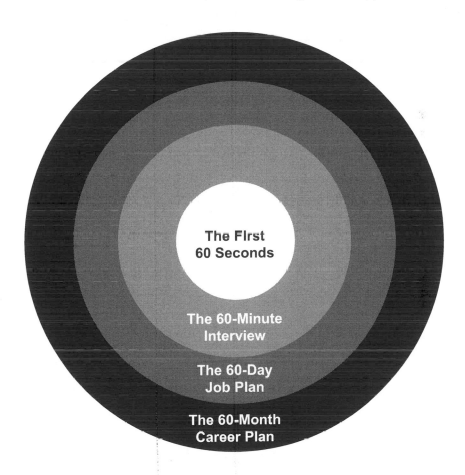

The First
60 Seconds

The 60-Minute
Interview

The 60-Day
Job Plan

The 60-Month
Career Plan

The chapters in this section cover the broad categories of activities you should focus on. We will delve into the details of each activity, including approach, execution, and timing. As you proceed through the chapters, keep in mind the 60-Day Plan Timeline, as referenced in Exhibit 1.2.

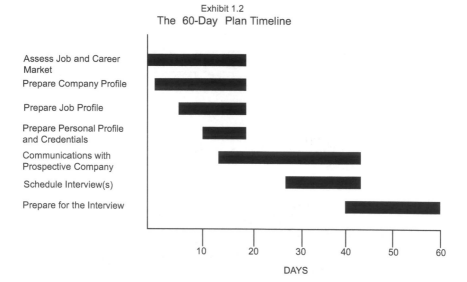

Exhibit 1.2
The 60-Day Plan Timeline

We will start this section by assessing the job market and expectations of companies and employers. Only by understanding how a prospective company hires a new employee will you be able to develop an effective plan. Additionally, we will look at options for assessing labor and market

Exhibit 1.3
Documentation Process Flow

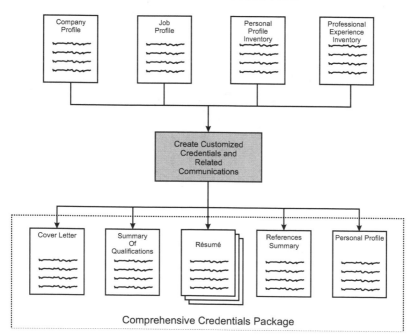

forces, local and national job markets, and specific strategies for identifying new career opportunities for you to consider.

The 60-Day Plan assists you in effectively managing the necessary documents and correspondence to make your career planning and job search efforts most effective. We will walk through the process of collecting the information and developing the profiles to customize your job search. Most people simply focus on writing a résumé. Our approach focuses first on collecting and preparing the necessary information so that your credentials will be the best possible. The Company Profile and Job Profile you prepare allow you to collect the information specific to the company and the job opportunity you may be interested in. The Personal Profile and Professional Experience Inventory give you the opportunity to effectively summarize your experience, strengths, and career aspirations.

As you can see in Exhibit 1.3, the profiles you develop will be used as inputs to your customized credentials and related correspondence. Completing the activities outlined in the 60-Day Plan will differentiate your application from most of your competition, simply because no one else will have done anything remotely similar. By investing a small amount of time in the preliminary stages, subsequent activities will be more easily achieved.

The last components of the 60-Day Plan focus on everything you need to do to arrange and prepare for the job interview.

CHAPTER 2

Assessing and Understanding Your Job and Career Market

As you can imagine, the business and employment landscape continually evolves in directions that are both supportive and challenging for the career-minded individual. It is worthwhile to spend the time up front to understand the overall market: the good and the bad, what is working and not working, and where the greatest opportunities lie.

Whether unemployment is up or down, whether the economy is doing well or not, there are always new job opportunities, and there is always competition for those jobs. You must focus on activities that differentiate you from the competition to win your desired career opportunity, regardless of market conditions.

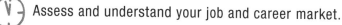 Assess and understand your job and career market.

Opportunities with Your Current Employer

Usually people think about getting a new job because they are not content with their current position. As a result, many people immediately think about opportunities at a new company. Most people assume that if they're not happy with their current employer, they never will be. If their employer has let their career reach a stalemate, the employer must not care or there must be something wrong. The person thinks: *if I haven't been given a new opportunity or the promotion I've been looking for, my company must not think too much of me.* Erase that from your mind. Do not assume that you have to look outside for your next great career opportunity. It may be right there, just waiting for you to ask for it. Of course, if you are not currently employed, we'll have to take a different approach, which we'll review in the next section.

If you are currently employed, regardless of position, your current employer should be your first step in evaluating career options. You have successes, experiences, and relationships with your employer that you should use to your advantage. While any prospective employer will be interested in those qualities, they will never mean as much as they do to your current employer. Your employer has invested in you, and unless you're a problem employee, they will want to keep you. It simply costs a company too much to lose a good employee.

You may not feel appreciated or respected for your talents and efforts, or it could be just the opposite and you're a key member of the team and your boss loves you. There could be dozens of reasons why you might be interested in a new career opportunity, and you need to first discuss those reasons with your current employer.

If your desire to make a change is related to positive factors, like wanting to expand the nature of your role and responsibilities or wanting to pursue a new career direction, it is very likely your current employer will be interested in helping you achieve your goals. It is very common for a company to assist an individual in changing departments and positions simply based on a positive history, a relationship, and a track record of success.

Maybe you are considering a new opportunity because you don't have a good working relationship with your current boss or a co-worker. That alone should not be a reason for you to leave a company. Good business leaders understand that sometimes people are just not in the right environment or the right position—that it's just not a "good fit." Those managers are open to discussing other opportunities for you. If your boss is not one of those people, find one good business leader you feel comfortable talking to within the company who can help you make a positive change, for the benefit of you and the company.

Whether your decision to pursue other opportunities is because of good or not-so-good reasons, start by assessing your options with your current employer. You have many options that can be evaluated and assessed easily and in short order while (or before) you evaluate the opportunities beyond. Below are several options to get started.

Schedule a meeting with your current boss or manager.

Whether formally or informally, the objective of the meeting is to share your career goals, how you plan to get there, how the company currently fits into your plans, and how you would like your career to develop in the next two to five years (we will focus on developing these plans in Chapter 28; page 234). Be prepared to share your past accomplishments and successes, your strengths, areas you are working on improving, and the career path you would like to take. If you feel a promotion or a job change is appropriate, *ask for it*. The most important thing for you to do is to *talk with your manager and let her know exactly how you feel*. If your boss doesn't know your aspirations and expectations, she cannot help you realize them. Too often, we're afraid to ask for what we want, or we think it will be a waste of time. It's mostly because we don't like confrontation, we're afraid of rejection, or we don't want to rock the boat. Make the effort. You have nothing to lose, and you might get exactly what you want.

Talk to your Human Resources department.

Most HR departments are concerned about the best interests of their employees. Many companies have an internal job posting process to provide career opportunities for current employees. It is to their advantage, and yours, for them to provide you with opportunities to keep you happy and satisfied, and to retain your knowledge and experience within the company. Ask to meet with the HR manager, and share your intentions with him or her. Evaluate any job openings that may be of interest and pursue them.

As a common courtesy, let your manager know if you are working with HR. It is best to be honest and up front when looking at opportunities within the company but outside of your area or department. Remember, if you're going to stay at your current company but work in a different department, your current boss will still be there. You never want to burn a bridge. If possible, work with your manager where he or she can be a positive reference and facilitator in obtaining another opportunity within the company.

Talk to associates, internal business customers, and others with whom you have worked closely in the past.

Use your past and current relationships to learn about other opportunities throughout the company. An internal business customer you have worked with in the past is always a great resource. Talk to anyone who knows of your personal and professional skills and who may benefit from your experience and knowledge. Someone may just step forward and offer you a job.

Continue to be a champion of the organization while you are there.

Business leaders and managers always react favorably to individuals who express an understanding of the company—its business and objectives— and who consistently support the company and display positive behaviors in the work environment. The reason is because it happens so infrequently. It's easy to criticize, more difficult to praise. Be positive, talk about the strengths of the company and its accomplishments, and how you and the company are going to be successful in the future. You'll be surprised how easily you can differentiate yourself from your co-workers and how favorably management will react.

 Continue to be a champion of the organization while pursuing a new career opportunity.

In summary, it is in your best interest to make the effort to land that next great job opportunity within your current company, before looking outside. Leaving a company is difficult—in many respects, you are starting over. Leaving means a new location and new transportation considerations. Most importantly, you may not be taking full advantage of the time you invested in the company and the experience and successes you acquired there, since those things will not mean as much to another company. Starting over can be a good thing, but if you can get everything you want and possibly more, give your current company a chance. Remember, your company has invested a lot in *you*. They really do want to keep you. Your job is to let them know how important you are to the future of the company. Help them make the decision to give you what you want and keep you with the organization.

Understanding the Employer's Viewpoint

It is important to understand how employers act and operate. What influences them? What motivates them? Exploring the employer's viewpoint makes you better prepared to interact effectively with potential employers.

Companies are genuinely interested in hiring the best people possible. They are looking for people who are interested in the particular business the company is engaged in and who have a good, solid work ethic. They want people who have the skills and experience to help the organization be more successful and accomplish its goals and objectives. Most of all, companies want people that have *desire* and *passion*. Everyone needs to work, and everyone wants to earn a good wage for a good day's work. But how many people work because they truly have a passion for what they do every day? How many people go to work every day and consistently show their desire to improve themselves and their companies? Not many. Employers are always on the lookout for these special people.

Employers look for desire and passion in many ways, most notably in the way you present yourself, which can be done through written and verbal communication as well as through body language. An employer wants to see how you really feel about your career—how important it is to you and how strongly you feel about being successful. The easiest way to do this is to express yourself with a never-ending combination of positive attitude and excitement. If you're excited about your career and can learn how to express that excitement, past successes come to light, future potential comes to the forefront, and your prospective employer will see you as a great all-around person who they would love to have as part of their organization.

At any given point in time, an organization has a myriad of challenges to address and overcome as it attempts to meet its defined goals and objectives. In efforts to build employee ranks with the best collection of skilled and experienced resources, organizations are often confronted with the challenge from a current or prospective employee: "What's in it for me?" This challenge can include everything from compensation and benefits concerns to career growth opportunities and promotion timelines—and every other employee-related issue that most managers do not enjoy dealing with. You do not want to be an additional challenge for your prospective employer. Instead, you will make the effort to learn about and understand the challenges the company is confronted with and you will prepare yourself to convey how you, as a new member of their team, will help them overcome those challenges. We'll talk more about how to do the necessary company research in the next chapter (page 18).

Human Resources as the "Gatekeeper"

The HR department is critical to helping build a strong workforce for an organization. They have broad authority and responsibilities and can be a valuable asset for the job seeker. The effective job seeker takes time to learn about a company's HR department. Depending on what you learn and your understanding of how a given organization's HR department functions, you can directly impact the overall process. Without the effort on your part, HR can also be the biggest obstacle in your efforts to get that next great job.

In most organizations, HR is responsible for the overall hiring objectives of the company. The members of this department are responsible for initiating and coordinating all of the open positions. In addition, they oversee the process of identifying and selecting potentially viable candidates and coordinating the interviewing and selection of candidates to fill the company's open positions. HR is critical to the success of the organization, helping to support and maintain the current employee ranks while adding to those ranks as necessary.

HR typically takes on the role of a gatekeeper, controlling and managing the overall number of opportunities available within an organization—the number of resources internal managers can or wish to hire. At the same time, HR controls the inflow of candidates interested in working for the company.

An HR department can find itself confronted with the following challenges:

- a need to understand the specific details of each and every available job opening;

- interaction with department managers who each have their own distinct expectations and time frames that may differ from the expectations of HR;

- a need to accommodate all internal employees interested in open positions (if an existing employee moves into a new job, HR is left with the open position for the employee who just transferred—one problem solved, a new one created);

- a large volume of résumés and inquiries that is extremely difficult to manage (in some cases, HR is left with no other option than to employ both technological and manual methods, as opposed to just manual review, to evaluate and select appropriate job candidates); and,

- sometimes overseeing the coordination of résumés with hiring managers, managing the interview and selection process, and overseeing the full hiring life cycle.

Knowing the role that HR plays in the overall process is critical to your approach. Take the initiative to understand HR's role for each company you may be interested in working for. The easiest and best way to do this is by simply calling a company's HR department and asking. They are usually more than happy to tell you how the process works.

Department Managers and Their Challenges

Department managers, like their HR counterparts, have specific goals and objectives that they need to achieve. They have projects to complete, budgets to manage, and customers to serve. While a department manager's goals and objectives should support the larger goals of HR and the organization as a whole, they tend to be narrower in scope. While HR plans consider the long-term perspective, department managers react to constant changes within the organization, the marketplace, and the workforce.

The department or hiring manager looking to hire an additional resource does not usually consider other hiring activities throughout the organization and is concerned solely with his individual hiring needs. He has his own expectations and time frames, which may or may not be aligned with the expectations and time frames of HR. This is important to note because if you are only following the direction of HR, and the hiring manager is not in agreement with one or more aspects of that direction, you may not meet everyone's expectations. It is important to know the role of HR *and* the hiring manager in the overall process. Here are some of the challenges department managers are confronted with in their efforts to hire a new employee:

- a need to obtain budget approvals, through a process that may be laborious and time consuming;

- a need to hire the new person immediately;

- unique knowledge of specific job requirements; and,

- a need to work with HR and sometimes other areas within the organization to hire a resource.

> **Note:** This last point can be viewed both positively and negatively by the hiring manager. On the positive side, if HR can handle much of the administrative process, then the hiring manager can focus on the interviewing and candidate selection. Conversely, some hiring managers would prefer full control over the candidate review, interviewing, selection, and hiring process, and may think other participants would hamper the process. Very often the hiring manager has his or her own specific process for evaluating and hiring a new resource that may or may not be in alignment with HR.

As the one ultimately responsible for the future of your career, you need to understand these challenges, expectations, and the sometimes differing expectations between hiring managers and HR in order to work with the hiring managers to meet your personal objectives.

Labor Supply and Market Forces

At any given time, there are a variety of market forces that can impact your efforts to make that next great career move. These labor or market forces impact organizations and their ability to effectively hire and maintain the level of employees required to support their business. Understanding these forces and their impact on the hiring process of an organization will put you in a much better position to effectively navigate through that process. You should consider:

- current hiring demands of corporations globally, locally, and within a given industry;

- current labor supplies, here and abroad;

- compensation trends; and,

- state of the local, regional, national, and global economies.

While these variables exist, don't spend time analyzing them or letting them impact your decision to make a change to further your career. These variables can and do impact job opportunities, but they have the most significant impact on the person who approaches a new job opportunity in the typical way. If you take the time to learn and implement the strategies in this book, you will be well prepared for any job opportunity in any type of job market.

To gain perspective on the market and labor forces that may impact your job search efforts, check national and local newspapers, which provide real-time assessment of employment, economic, and overall business conditions. The best resource that I have found that provides the broadest scope of data is the U.S. Department of Labor, Bureau of Labor Statistics (www.bls.gov), which provides a wealth of information on employment and unemployment conditions, prices and living conditions, occupations, compensation and working conditions, productivity and technology, and employment projections.

Identifying Suitable Opportunities

With recent technological developments and the proliferation of services geared toward the job seeker, the ability to identify suitable opportunities is easier than ever. Below are some general avenues for exposing yourself to new career opportunities. (We will go over detailed strategies in Chapter 29; page 246.)

- Job search websites can target specific opportunities in specific geographic areas. Such sites often allow you to register and make your credentials available so hiring companies can find you.

- Job placement organizations provide services for individuals in a broad range of categories, from executive to temporary positions.

- Company-specific websites provide detailed information about the company, available positions, and the employment process.

- Industry associations, user groups, and labor groups provide excellent exposure to the people and resources that can help support your career plans.

- Also look for standard employment advertising methods, including newspaper and online classifieds, company and group job fairs, etc.

While the resources available for identifying suitable career opportunities may seem endless and overwhelming, with a little research and exploration, the job search will become manageable. Do your best to make use of a broad scope of resources. The broader the scope, the greater the potential for uncovering more opportunities.

CHAPTER 3

The Company Profile

Once you have identified one or more job opportunities to pursue, it's time to do a little research. First, we will start by researching the company that has the job opportunity you are interested in, and in the next chapter (page 23), we will prepare a more complete and comprehensive job profile.

You're probably wondering: *why should I research the company?*

First, researching the company allows you to determine if you really want to work there. Better to get this information early in your job search process before you spend too much time pursuing a job at a company you don't want to work for.

Second, interviewers and hiring managers want to know that you're really interested in the job and in the company as a whole. They want you to know as much about the company as they do. They want to know that you've made an effort to understand the company, the business, and the work environment. Although interviewers want job candidates to research their company, many people don't make an effort to do so.

This fact is a great differentiator—which is exactly why you are going to do it. By preparing a brief profile of the company you may soon be working for, you will gain the following:

- a basic understanding of the company's history;

- the ability to provide a one- to two-sentence summary of the primary business the company is engaged in;

- an understanding of the company's primary competition;

- an understanding of the company's current financial situation;

- an assessment of the outlook for the industry; and,

- knowledge of the nature of the work environment.

You want to acquire this information as you begin your job search so that you do not have to worry about it later, during an interview. The last thing you want to do is use up valuable interview time talking about the history of the company or benefit details. If you start off armed with knowledge of the company, that lets the prospective company's interviewer or hiring manager know that you've made an effort; you know about the company at a sufficient level of detail. That knowledge shows you really want to work at the company.

Prepare a Company Profile for every company you are interested in.

Preparing the Company Profile

Please refer to and use the Company Profile Template in Exhibit 3.1 on page 21.

The Company Profile Template, like other templates and activities provided in the book, is designed to provide the most benefit with the most reasonable investment of your time. In many cases, the Company Profile can be completed within two hours. You can spend more or less time as your schedule permits, but keep this in mind: any time you spend preparing your Company Profile is more than your competition will be spending to learn about the company (usually 50–100 percent more time). The more time you spend, the more you will differentiate yourself with your prospective employer.

Most of the information you need will be available from the company's website. If it's not available there, call the HR department. Additionally, see if you can find someone who has worked at the company before, which can be accomplished through networking and online forums. For industry information and other financial and business information, there are an extensive number of resources available. The following is a general list of some of the resources:

- Visit the website of any financial management or brokerage company.

- Research industry trade organizations, which are created to support the employees and employers of most industries. Using any online search engine, enter your particular industry name followed by "trade organization" to obtain a listing of organizations for you to research.

- For public companies, try the Securities and Exchange Commission (SEC)—www.sec.gov.

- Online news search services exist for all major national and local newspapers. News services have online search capabilities through their websites and can provide extensive amount of current and archived information about a company you are interested in.

- Visit your local library and ask a librarian for help. Let the librarian know that you want to discover everything you can about a given company, specifically the information on your Company Profile Template (have an extra copy to give the librarian).

Before you go any further, take time now to complete a Company Profile for any company you are considering.

Exhibit 3.1
Company Profile Template

Company Name: XYZ Company

General Corporate Information:

       Headquarters
       Address   _____

                                      _____

       City, State, Zip   _____

       Primary Phone Number   _____

       HR Contact & Phone No.   _____

       Website Address   _____

       Name of CEO   _____

Brief Corporate History:

Primary Business Company Is Engaged In (no more than two sentences):

Industry Category: _____

Industry Outlook:

Exhibit 3.1
Company Profile Template

Primary Competitors and Market % (top 3):	Company XYZ	% _____
	_____	% _____
	_____	% _____
	_____	% _____

Financial Summary:	Current Year	Prior Year
Revenue	_____	_____
Net Income	_____	_____

Work Environment:

Flexible Work Hours	☐ Yes	☐ No	
Type	☐ Professional	☐ Casual	☐ Other_____
Work Location	☐ Office	☐ Field	☐ Other_____

Employee Benefits Summary:

Compensation	☐ Salary	☐ Hourly	☐ Bonus
	☐ Commission	☐ Other_____	
401(k)	☐ Yes	☐ No	
Matching Contribution	☐ Yes	☐ No	% _____
Vacation	☐ 1 Week	☐ 2 weeks	☐ Other_____
Sick Time	☐ 1 Week	☐ 2 weeks	☐ Other_____
Insurance	☐ Health	☐ Dental	☐ Life
	☐ S/T Disability	☐ L/T Disability	☐ Other_____

Other Key Benefits	_____
	_____
	_____

CHAPTER 4

The Job Profile

The Job Profile is a critical, yet often overlooked aspect of the job search and assessment process. It is similar to a Company Profile but helps you gather detailed information about a specific job or position at a company. It is critical because if you do not obtain the details suggested, it will be difficult to ensure that the position meets your expectations, desires, and career objectives.

The Job Profile is usually left out because people take the path of least resistance, trying to get by with the least possible effort. Typically, job seekers can get basic information about a job or position through a website, job board, or a variety of other avenues. With this information, they make a snap judgment about whether it is a suitable opportunity or not.

But I know that's not you.

From now on, you will take this process a step further. You should formally document everything and ensure that you have all the necessary information to make an informed decision. You also want to formally think about and document how your experience matches the available opportunity and begin thinking about how you'll convince your potential employer that you are the best person for the job.

Prepare a Job Profile for each and every job opportunity that you seriously consider for these important reasons:

- It allows you to develop a comprehensive understanding of the position: the company's expectations, responsibilities of the role, and how the position fits into the bigger picture of the organization's primary business endeavors.

- It provides clarity and detail regarding the skills and experience required for the position.

- It allows you to quantify and qualify your skills and experience relative to the position to help you determine if the job is indeed a "fit."

- It provides the opportunity to quantify the positive and negative aspects of the position.

- It allows you to perform a quick assessment of the position relative to your goals, expectations, and desires.

- It provides you with a comprehensive understanding of the position that will be unlike anything your competition has prepared.

 Prepare a Job Profile for each and every position you are considering.

The Job Profile gives you the ability to assess the particular job opportunity and make an informed decision about whether to pursue the opportunity or not. Without taking the time to complete the profile, you risk spending valuable time chasing a job or position that is not suitable for you.

Please refer to the Job Profile Template in Exhibit 4.1 on page 26. You will collect the following information:

- position title, grade level, location, and compensation package;

- brief description of the position;

- primary skills required; and,

- primary job responsibilities.

Next, you will make a few objective and subjective qualifications regarding any potentially positive or negative aspects. Positive aspects include any particular characteristic of the position that you feel makes it a good fit for your future career plans and expectations—and it can be anything at all. A negative aspect makes you uncomfortable about working in such a position or role. At this point in your research, there should be no limits, and you should consider everything. You have to determine if the negative aspects are really issues for you, if you are willing to accept them, or if you feel it is possible to overcome them. Maybe the negative aspects are minor and can be easily justified and overshadowed by the positive aspects. Focus on identifying as many positive aspects as possible—you want to have dozens of reasons for pursuing your next opportunity. If you are unable to come up with at least five positive aspects, maybe your time would be better spent on another opportunity.

After completing the profile, if you still feel that the opportunity is worth pursuing, relate your most recent experiences to the position requirements and expectations. As a rule of thumb, you want to share with your prospective employer your most recent five years of experience and explain how those recent experiences are relevant to what they may be looking for. For now, try to identify three to five specific experiences in the last five years that closely match the expectations of the position.

Once you have completed both the Company Profile and the Job Profile, you'll find you can use them in tandem. Both profiles will assist you in preparing your credentials and related job search documentation. As your understanding of the position and expectations become clearer, you'll be able to let your prospective employer know how you feel about the position. Your collection of positive aspects will be used to convince yourself that the position is right for you—a good match in terms of job type and required qualifications.

Before you go any further, take time now to review and finalize your Job Profile for any position you are seriously considering.

Exhibit 4.1
Job Profile Template

Company Name: XYZ Company

Position Summary:

    Position Title   _____

    Information Sources   ☐ Company Site   ☐ Classifieds

                              ☐ Online Job Search ☐ Other_____

    Grade Level   _____

    Compensation   ☐ Salary   ☐ Hourly   ☐ Bonus

                              ☐ Commission ☐ Other_____

                              $_____

    Department/Location   _____

    Hiring Manager   _____

Brief Description of the Position:

```
┌──────────────────────────────────────────────────┐
│                                                    │
│                                                    │
│                                                    │
│                                                    │
│                                                    │
└──────────────────────────────────────────────────┘
```

                                                           Have?

Primary Skills Required: _____   ☐

                                   _____   ☐

                                   _____   ☐

                                   _____   ☐

                                   _____   ☐

Primary Job Responsibilities: _____

                                   _____

                                   _____

                                   _____

Exhibit 4.1
Job Profile Template

Top 3 Relevant Experiences I Have

Experience 1: _____

_____

Experience 2: _____

_____

Experience 3: _____

_____

Top 3 Positive Aspects of the Position

Positive 1: _____

_____

Positive 2: _____

_____

Positive 3: _____

_____

Top 3 Negative Aspects of the Position

Issue?

Negative 1: _____ ☐

_____

Negative 2: _____ ☐

_____

Negative 3: _____ ☐

_____

CHAPTER 5

Your Personal Profile

Now we'll talk about one of the most important and influential documents that you can prepare to differentiate yourself: your Personal Profile. The Personal Profile outlines for you initially—and ultimately for your prospective employer—all of your unique personal qualities. Refer to and use the Personal Profile Inventory in Exhibit 5.1 on page 32.

The Personal Profile has nothing to do with your work-related experience and everything to do with who you are as a person—what makes you unique and different from everyone else. The profile reveals your passions, your hobbies, and what makes you tick. Specifically, you should develop a Personal Profile for yourself that includes at least the following:

- your passions;

- hobbies and special interests;

- personal development activities;

- family; and,

- other unique or interesting qualities about yourself.

The Personal Profile is all about differentiation, and no one else is doing it. This is a small, incremental, and additional effort that can make you stand out above the competition and increase your chances of getting that new career opportunity you certainly deserve.

If you have the opportunity to meet with a hiring manager, his or her objective will be to observe you and discern "who you are" to qualify you as a prospective job candidate. Why not provide the hiring manager the opportunity to observe you, so to speak, before you ever meet? Your challenge is to assist the hiring manager in understanding who *you* really are in an effective and positive manner, both before and during the job interview. The Personal Profile helps you accomplish that.

But what if you never get the opportunity to meet the manager? If used effectively, you can use the Personal Profile to help your prospective employer gain a full understanding of all your important nonwork and personal qualities *in addition* to your work experience and qualifications as early in the process as possible. Think about it. A hiring manager has very specific needs and attempts to assess the qualifications of interested candidates to find the one that best suits his or her needs. This is initially done by reviewing a batch of résumés, in some cases a very large batch, and making a qualification on each résumé to determine who to include in the interview process. You want to—and need to—provide more for the manager to consider.

Prepare a Personal Profile of your unique personal qualities.

Let's highlight the reasons why the Personal Profile is important:

1. You *are more than your "work."*

   You are so much more than what could possibly show up on a résumé. If others prefer to be considered, judged, and selected based solely on their work experience, let them. You will make the additional effort to go beyond what everyone else is doing. You are going to make it personal.

2. *It's all about relationships, and it's always personal.*

   Work is work. You have a job to do, and day in and day out you will do that job, as will everyone else. But in performing your daily job, you will most likely be interacting with people. You may end up spending more time with your boss and co-workers than you will with your friends and family. Positive relationships make that situation tolerable and even downright enjoyable. If you want that new career opportunity, you have to convince your prospective employer that you bring positive personal qualities to the work environment.

3. *It's all about differentiation.*

The Personal Profile allows you to differentiate yourself from every other person being considered for a given opportunity. You are unique—let them know it. Even if everyone reads this book and everyone starts preparing similar profiles for consideration, none will be exactly like yours. A hiring manager may have difficulty choosing between two candidates with similar work experiences, but the personal information you provide will always be unique and different.

4. *Let them know* now *who you are.*

You want your prospective employer to know exactly what—and who—they are getting. Even if you have the opportunity to meet with your prospective employer, you usually don't get into this topic during an interview. Why should they wait until six months after you're hired to find out what a great and interesting person you are? Let them know now.

5. *Your personal qualities are as important as your work experience.*

Equally important (and sometimes more so) to your prior work experience or training, your unique personal qualities determine how you will approach a given job, how you will interact with others to meet objectives, and ultimately how successful you will be.

6. *It always comes back to* you.

In addition to aiding the employer in understanding who you are, the Personal Profile is also extremely important in helping you determine if a given opportunity is right for you. By identifying and understanding all of your personal qualities, it will help you evaluate and select career opportunities best suited for you.

Completing the Personal Profile

We will begin the process of completing the Personal Profile by first taking a step back and looking at the many individual characteristics that make you interesting. The idea is to brainstorm as many unique personal attributes as possible. We will then use some of that information to prepare the profile.

Exhibit 5.1 is a Personal Profile Inventory that guides you through the types of questions you want to ask yourself and think about. It is a data collection tool to assist you in acquiring a breadth of personal information for use in your Personal Profile. As you complete the inventory, keep the following in mind:

- This is a brainstorming exercise. Try to write down as many items as possible without analyzing them in any way and without any constraints whatsoever.

- The only rule is don't think about your past work experience.

- Feel free to come up with additional questions.

- Don't hesitate to ask friends and family what they think.

After completing the inventory, you should have a couple pages of all the things that make you great. Your next challenge will be to review, summarize, and consolidate those items into a one-page, clear and concise summary of all your best characteristics. Take the opportunity now to complete your Personal Profile Inventory.

Having completed your Personal Profile Inventory, try to categorize each item you listed as either (1) passions, (2) hobbies and special interests, (3) personal development activities, (4) family, and (5) other unique or interesting qualities. Categorizing your inventory makes it easier to incorporate your personal attributes in a more formal Personal Profile document.

Exhibit 5.1
Personal Profile Inventory

- List the top five things you like to do when you are not working.

- Outside of work, what are you truly passionate about? List three things that you cannot live without, that you love more than anything, and explain why you are so passionate about them.

- List any hobbies you have.

- List any athletic activities you participate in.

- Describe your family.

- Do you have any special talents?

- Do you now or have you ever played a musical instrument? If so, explain what and when. If not, if you were to take up learning to play an instrument today, what would it be?

- Do you like to read? If so, what type of books do you read?

- Are you affiliated with any religious, charitable, or member organizations?

- List three characteristics about yourself you feel you can improve upon. How would you go about making that happen?

- How would your closest friend describe you?

- Do you have any pets?

- Do you like to travel? Where is your favorite place that you have been to, and where do you hope to go next?

- What is your educational background? What was your greatest learning experience?

- Are you currently engaged in any continuing education programs or do you have any planned?

With all of your ideas identified, written down, and categorized, it is now time to complete your Personal Profile. As your prepare your profile, your focus will be on the following:

- personal differentiation;

- selling your strengths; and,

- selling your weaknesses, or as I like to refer to them, your areas in need of improvement.

Exhibit 5.2 on page 35 is an example of a Personal Profile that I prepared for myself. Let's review that example.

- We start off with *passion*, which is what life is all about. Everyone says they love their work, but aside from that, what are you really passionate about?

- I know what you're thinking. My number one passion is writing, and that's work. All I can say is that since I've become a writer, I haven't worked a single day. It's pure passion, pure joy, and it's all fun.

- For each category, pull from your inventory the top two or three items that you feel strongest about. For each of those items, write a one-sentence description that succinctly conveys your quality.

- You may also be wondering why family is at the bottom of the list. For me, my family comes first and is the most important thing in my life. But that's true for you and everyone else. Since family will not necessarily differentiate you from everyone else, I moved it to the bottom. If someone were to ask me about it in an interview, I would say that I saved the best for last.

- Also keep in mind that this is *your* Personal Profile. Depending on how your profile develops, rearrange the order or the format to best sell *you*.

- The section on Personal Development is extremely important. Sure, you want to, and need to, stress your best positive qualities. At the same time, no one is perfect and everyone has the ability to improve and develop. Take a long, hard look at yourself and identify at least two areas you would like to improve or further develop and plan how you might go about it. The ability to realize a shortcoming and take the initiative to overcome it is a tremendous asset. Include this in your profile.

- The Personal Profile is one page in length—nothing more. This will make more sense as we prepare your credentials in Chapter 7 (page 43); we want to make sure that each component of your credentials package (your Personal Profile included) is efficient and effective in presentation and communication.

- Finally, I can assure you that there is not one person in this world who has exactly the same personal profile as me.

After you have completed your Personal Profile, set it aside and let it rest for a day. Then go back and review it again. Once you're comfortable with it, show it to someone you respect and trust, and ask them what they think. Let them view it not only from their perspective but ask them to review it from the perspective of a hiring manager. Make any last revisions, and you're done. For now, set it aside, along with the Company and Job Profiles (we use all three in Chapter 7; page 43).

Exhibit 5.2
Personal Profile Example

Personal Profile for Dan Burns

My Passions

- Writing

    I enjoy writing on a daily basis. There is nothing more rewarding than getting the words, the paragraphs, and the stories down onto the page and then in retrospect wondering where it all came from.

- Playing Guitar

    I took guitar lessons as a young boy, followed by thirty years of air guitar performance. The real guitar is back, and I'm learning to play all the songs I love.

- Fly-Fishing

    There is nothing better than being in the middle of nowhere, knee-deep in river, and hearing only the sound of the rushing water—it's heaven.

My Hobbies and Special Interests

- Book Reading and Collecting

    I love all genres of fiction but particularly enjoy mysteries and science fiction.

- Fly-Tying

    My love of fly-fishing includes tying my own flies and coming up with new insect imitations (so I can outfish my best friend Gerry).

Personal Development Activities

- Guitar and Music Lessons

    In my pursuit of rock-and-roll greatness, I take weekly guitar lessons at the local music store and make every effort to practice four to five times a week.

- Writing Development

    I have so much to learn about developing as a fiction writer. I write a thousand words a day and read two writing books a month.

- Personal Goal

    To have a collection of my short stories published and to one day adapt one of those stories into a screenplay. There is a novel in there somewhere as well.

My Family

- Married with two children; a sixteen-year-old daughter and eleven-year-old son.
- We try to spend every weekend together at the lake—fishing, boating, playing games, and just hanging out.

CHAPTER 6

Your Professional Experience Inventory

Going to the Vault...and It's Locked

We have all had the same experience. The time has come to prepare or update your résumé, and you're under extreme duress to get it done as quickly as possible. A new job opportunity has presented itself and you need to send off a résumé first thing in the morning. You sit down at your desk and pull out the résumé you used the last time. When was that, five years ago? You scan your professional experience, starting with the oldest, and what you read seems distant and vague, like it describes a person you don't even know. If you are a student heading into the professional world for the first time, you are equally challenged. *What was that class I took? I wish I could remember the person I worked for during my internship.*

So you sit back in your chair, and go deep into the recesses of your mind, into that vault containing everything you tried to remember but thought that you would never need again. You search for something, anything even remotely relevant or useful to add to your résumé. Most times it just doesn't come.

The Professional Experience Inventory is the tool you will use, starting today, that will prevent you from ever being in that position again. Preparing the inventory will make it easy for you to update your résumé and clearly and effectively communicate your past accomplishments and successes.

The Professional Experience Inventory in Perspective

The Professional Experience Inventory is a simple and straightforward one-page document of the most critical and relevant information about your work experiences. In Exhibit 6.1 on page 42 you will find a template of the Professional Experience Inventory for you to review and use. You will detail your current job, and you will also go back and accumulate details about prior experiences.

When I first began my career, I had a manager who suggested, and even indirectly mandated, that I keep a log of every significant vocational activity and project I worked on. His explanation seemed logical enough; he said that it would be difficult to go back over a long period of time and remember everything significant—or maybe not so significant—that may have happened. He went on to suggest that we would use my collected information at my performance appraisal to see what I actually accomplished. I was young and impressionable and I listened to him, even though at the time I thought it was nothing more than a lot of administrative busy work.

For the next twelve months, I took fifteen minutes each month to update my work experience log. It was easy to remember what happened in the past month and the time spent updating the information was insignificant. When it came time for my first annual performance appraisal, I brought my work experience log with me. My manager was quite pleased, and to be honest I was quite surprised myself at everything that I had accomplished over the year. As we reviewed the pages, there were many things I had completely forgotten about. But the experiences were all there, in writing, as a complete and factual record of my year of effort. I walked out of my manager's office with a near perfect performance appraisal and the maximum salary increase allowable. The three hours I spent over the year updating my work experience log provided an exceptional return on investment.

The point of the story and the reason you will be preparing a Professional Experience Inventory is that there is a real benefit to taking a proactive approach to managing your career. It's the principle that this entire book is based on. Do things now, before you really need to and before the other pressures of life and time constraints settle in. Take care of business before it needs to be taken care of.

Do it because no one else is doing it. Do it to be different. It will pay off in the end.

🕐 Prepare and maintain a Professional Experience Inventory.

Preparing the Professional Experience Inventory

Before we go through the inventory and describe the components of it, let me answer a couple of questions you may be asking yourself.

Why don't I just prepare the inventory when I prepare or update my résumé?

When it's time for you to prepare or update your résumé, it will probably be too late—you won't remember everything necessary. Second, and more importantly, your objective is to prepare a comprehensive and documented record of your work experience. When we prepare your résumé in the next chapter (page 43), you will find that we won't use everything in the inventory for the customized résumé you prepare for your next opportunity. You may end up using some information now and some later for a much different opportunity. You want a more detailed level of information to draw upon when you prepare your résumé.

Are there any other types of information I can include?

The template allows you to effectively pull together the most critical information you need. It also seamlessly supports the résumé creation process that we discuss in the next chapter. Having said that, you can collect and document any information that might be helpful in conveying your experience to a prospective employer. I like to keep my inventories to one page for each job position that I have had. The one-page limit forces me to focus on just the most important information and keeps it manageable. But remember the reason you're doing this: to proactively document your experience and accomplishments now, so you can easily and effectively prepare your résumé later. If that means going beyond one page and including other categories, go for it. It's just another differentiator you can use to your advantage later.

When exactly should I prepare my Professional Experience Inventory?

Do it right now; don't wait any longer. If this is your first time preparing an inventory, you will have to invest a little time up front. Prepare an inventory sheet for each employer and each position you held at that employer. Start with your most recent experience and work backward, preparing inventories going back no more than five years. Employers are most interested in your recent and relevant experiences, and going back five years is a reasonable time frame.

After you have prepared your five-year inventory, update your current experience inventory on a periodic basis to keep it fresh and accurate. You don't have to do it monthly like I did, but at a minimum I suggest you update it every three months. Put a reminder in your schedule and spend fifteen minutes updating your inventory when prompted. You will also want to create a new inventory with each new job opportunity you encounter.

Professional Experience Inventory Section by Section

Let's take a moment to go through each section of the Professional Experience Inventory template (Exhibit 6.1, on page 42), and explain its purpose, focus, and benefits.

Position Summary

In this section you document the relevant details of the position. As mentioned earlier, prepare a new inventory each time you change job roles. This information provides for a base experience and compensation history. **Note:** Remember that the inventory can be used to document your internship or work-study experience as well.

General Description

In no more than two sentences, describe the position. Be clear and concise, and describe it as if you were trying to attract someone to fill the role, as though it were the greatest opportunity in the world.

Key Accomplishments

Identify the top five or six accomplishments you have realized in this role. This is a section where you can feel free to go beyond the space provided in the template. If the accomplishment is significant to you, write it down. All accomplishments are good.

Primary Job Responsibilities

Identify your top four job responsibilities. Focus on those things you are responsible for, not simply what you do every day at work. Employers are interested in responsibilities you are entrusted with, not specific activities you may perform on a daily basis.

What I Learned and How I Developed

This can be the most important section of all. You want to continually learn and develop as you progress with your career. If you find this section difficult, it may be time to talk with your manager to discuss learning and development opportunities. It is extremely important to share with your current and prospective employer how your job or experience helped you grow and develop both personally and professionally. You also want to share any internal or external advanced learning or educational activities you may have pursued.

Key Skills

Identify the primary business, technical, interpersonal, or other skills you used to effectively realize your accomplishments and satisfy or meet your responsibilities.

References

I can't tell you how many times someone told me they didn't have the name or contact information of the person they worked for, or how many times I was given personal references instead of professional references. Your prospective employer is interested in what your past boss or direct customer thinks of you. That is the primary point of this section: to identify one manager that you report directly to, and one customer that you work directly with. You want as much contact information as possible because you are going to provide it as part of your credentials package. Also, write down what you feel they would say about you, and don't be afraid to quote your manager or customer directly.

How You Will Use the Professional Experience Inventory

All of the information you gather will help prepare your résumé. You can very easily transfer information from your inventory directly to related sections on your résumé. You will have a lot of information to draw from and you can customize your résumé for each new opportunity.

Also, you can use your experience inventory at your next performance appraisal with your current boss. Because of your efforts, you can provide detailed and factual information relating to how you met and exceeded your goals and expectations, which will put you in an excellent position for negotiating that next promotion or compensation increase.

This concludes our efforts to pull together all of your background information and research. In the next chapter, you will use your collected information to put together a professional and comprehensive credentials package unlike anything your competition may be preparing. Get ready to differentiate yourself.

Exhibit 6.1
Professional Experience Inventory

Company Name: XYZ Company

Period of Time in Position: MM/DD/YYYY through MM/DD/YYYY

Position Summary:

    Position Title/Grade Level: _____
    Compensation: _____
    Location: _____

Brief Description of the Position:

Key Accomplishments: _____
                             _____
                             _____
                             _____
                             _____

Primary Job Responsibilities: _____
                             _____
                             _____
                             _____
                             _____

What I Learned and
How I Developed: _____
                             _____
                             _____
                             _____

Key Skills: _____
                             _____
                             _____
                             _____

References: *Direct Manager*
                             Name _____
                             Title _____
                             Phone and Email _____
                             What would they say about you?_____

                             Primary Customer
                             Name _____
                             Title _____
                             Phone and Email _____
                             What would they say about you?_____

CHAPTER 7

Preparing Your Credentials

Now You're Ready!

Now that you have prepared everything you need regarding the prospective company you are interested in, the particular job opportunity, and your personal information, you are ready to prepare your credentials.

In this chapter we focus on preparing a complete credentials package to effectively sell *you* to a prospective employer. You will notice that I have not used the word "résumé" yet. I use the term "credentials" because it is significantly broader in scope—the résumé is only one part of it. Throughout the chapter, we will define and describe the other differentiating components of your credentials, including your résumé. In its entirety, your complete credentials package will not only set you apart from your competition, it will make it significantly easier for your prospective employer to identify you as the candidate of choice and select you for the opportunity you deserve.

Prepare a comprehensive credentials package, not simply a résumé, to answer all of the questions your prospective employer may have—before they ask them.

Before we get into the different components, let me tell you how this broader concept of "credentials" came about. In my past experience managing a company that provided consulting services to *Fortune* 500 clients, I coordinated and participated in hundreds of job interviews. I presented résumés of staff consultants to clients and allowed them to review the experience of the consultant and interview them before deciding to engage them on a project. During the interview process, it was a rare occurrence that an interviewer did not make a request for additional information. It was common for the interviewee to hear, "Do you have any professional references?" or "What do you know about our company?" or "Can you provide more details of your most recent experience?" As you can imagine, the list of questions can go on and on. Frustrated that I could not get a firm commitment after an interview, my focus turned to how I could answer all of the questions for clients before they even asked them. Your credentials will focus on satisfying that objective as well.

In many cases a job seeker receives no response after submitting his or her résumé for an opportunity. This is extremely frustrating for the job seeker, yet as I spoke with the hiring managers I worked with, I quickly understood why they do not always respond. It is too difficult for a hiring manager to easily differentiate your résumé from everyone else's. It's as simple as that. Sure, there are a thousand different ways to format a résumé, but it's still just a résumé. We'll talk about a number of areas to focus on when preparing your résumé and certain formatting suggestions, but we'll spend the rest of the time talking about the other components of your credentials package—all of the other pieces hiring managers don't typically see. These pieces will set you apart from other candidates and answer all of the hiring manager's questions (and more).

Objectives of Well-Prepared Credentials

Let's define a set of objectives for you to keep in mind as you prepare credentials.

- Share your knowledge and understanding about the prospective company and the specific opportunity available.

- Efficiently and effectively convey your *recent* and *relevant* professional experience.

- Let the interviewer know who you are as a person.

- Let the interviewer know other people hold a high opinion of you.

- Focus on *differentiation*—tell your prospective employer how and why you are different from anyone else.

- State specifically why you are the best person for the job.

- Make it *easy* for your prospective employer to select you.

Your Credentials Package

Let's take a moment to refer again to the Documentation Process Flow we discussed earlier.

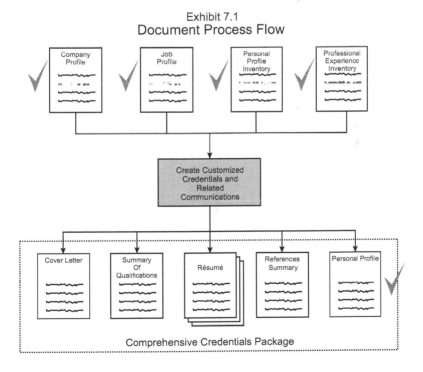

Exhibit 7.1
Document Process Flow

In the four previous chapters, we focused on acquiring and preparing detailed information about the company, the job opportunities, your key personal attributes, and your professional experience. Now we'll use the information collected in each of those steps to prepare the following components of your credentials package:

- Cover Letter and Summary of Qualifications

- Résumé

- References Summary

The Five Key Points to Document Formatting and Production

A lack of attention to some basic formatting and production details can detract from your content and even render what you have prepared useless.

1. *Document setup*

   When formatting your pages, use a standard one-inch margin on all sides.

2. *Font*

   Don't use artsy or nonstandard fonts to differentiate you from others, as many times this can backfire. Use a standard, legible, and professional-looking font, twelve point in size. Arial and Times New Roman are most suitable.

3. *Standard electronic format*

   Use an industry-standard electronic format when preparing your documents. All your hard work will be wasted if your prospective employer cannot open and read what you have prepared. Speak with someone at the company or check a company's website for formats they accept. Most companies usually accept Microsoft Word and Adobe PDF formats.

4. *Paper*

   The use of high-end paper can differentiate you and express professionalism. Ninety-nine percent of your competition will be using standard 20-lb. white printer paper. Use a heavier bond paper, and don't be afraid to venture outside the standard white. The quality and brightness of the heavier bond papers are noticeable, and subtle off-white colors can make your credentials stand out while staying within the boundaries of what is reasonably acceptable. If you use a non-white paper, remain conservative and stay within the various shades of white.

5. *Be consistent*

   Most importantly, practice consistency throughout all of the documents you prepare. Remember, this is a credentials package. Use these guidelines to ensure that your credentials are perceived as a professional, cohesive whole.

The Cover Letter

The purpose of the cover letter, which is always required, is to put an enticing front page and attention grabber on your credentials package, and to convey what is included in your credentials. The cover letter is the first thing your prospective employer will see and read, so it needs to be clear, concise, effective, and noticeably (but not obnoxiously) different. As suggested below, include specific details to make the cover letter stand out and grab the interest of the reader.

- Show that you have extensively researched the company and are knowledgeable about the business.

- State the specific position you are interested in and why.

- Reference the Summary of Qualifications and how your qualifications match the position's requirements.

- Reference your included résumé, Personal Profile, and References Summary.

- Ask for the opportunity to meet in person.

Exhibit 7.2 on page 55 shows an example of a standard cover letter.

The Summary of Qualifications

When I was a hiring manager with an open position to fill, I found that I had a difficult time getting through all the résumés submitted for consideration, even after they were pre-screened by the HR department. There were just too many. If I could spare the time to go through all of them in their entirety, which was not usually the case, I still had difficulty trying to distinguish one résumé from the next. The different résumé formats made it difficult to identify and pull out the details I was looking for.

Hiring managers today are confronted with similar challenges. What you don't want to have happen is for someone to review your résumé, overlook or misinterpret your experience and qualifications, and eliminate you from consideration.

The Summary of Qualifications addresses that potential problem for the HR department or hiring manager. It is different from a résumé in that it provides a clear, concise, and customized assessment of your professional experience (found in your résumé) and personal attributes (from your Personal Profile) and how that experience and those attributes align *specifically* with the objectives of the organization and the requirements of the position. The Summary of Qualifications provides this in a greater level of detail than provided in your cover letter. After you pique the hiring manager's interest with your cover letter, you save him the time of going through the details of your résumé and provide qualitative, objective, and definitive reasons why you are the best person for the job.

Prepare a Summary of Qualifications for your prospective employer to give them a customized summary of your professional experience, personal attributes, and specifically why you are the best person for the job.

Preparing the Summary of Qualifications

Let's go through each of the four sections of the Summary of Qualifications and discuss how to prepare them. Refer to Exhibit 7.3 on page 56 for a Summary of Qualifications template. Note the straightforward one-page format. The goal is to make your points definitively and with supporting qualitative statements.

The statements below are clear and direct. You can use these or others you may come up with. The important point is to clearly state to your prospective employer, *with conviction and confidence*, why you should be selected for the job. If done right, the Summary of Qualifications may be all the hiring manager needs to select you for the position or as an interview candidate.

I understand the expectations of the company and the position.

Draw from information included in both the Company Profile and Job Profile. Your prospective employer will be impressed by your initiative and understanding; it's not something he or she normally sees.

I have very recent and relevant experience.

In this section, draw from your Professional Experience Inventory to highlight specific *recent and relevant* experiences, accomplishments, and responsibilities related to the open position.

I have personal, nonwork attributes that will prove valuable to my success in this role.

Here is where you summarize your great nonwork qualities from your Personal Profile. Let the potential employer know that the job is more than just a job—that it is not only a career choice for you, but that it is also an important part of your life, that it is personal. Show your prospective employer how your personal attributes will be an asset to the organization.

I want to be an integral part of the continued future success of XYZ Corporation.

Drawing from the Company Profile again, state your understanding of the company's mission, goals, plans, and industry outlook, and why that is exciting or of interest to you.

Preparing Your Résumé

Completing your résumé should be simple if you have done your homework and completed the Professional Experience Inventory process and Personal Profile. If you have not, return to the previous chapters to complete the preparation of these important supporting materials.

As you prepare a résumé, keep in mind the following considerations:

- The résumé format should follow the same characteristics as the rest of the documents in your credentials package. Refer back to the format guidelines discussed earlier in the chapter.

- Keep your résumé to three pages total. Going beyond that length typically provides no additional benefit and can sometimes have a negative impact. Remember, you want to make it manageable for the person reviewing the résumé, and you do not want your résumé overlooked or discarded because the hiring manager does not want to go through the trouble of reading an excessive number of pages.

- In preparing job-specific details, include experiences that are most recent and relevant.

- *Customize* the résumé for each company/job opportunity you are interested in.

With your Personal Profile and Professional Experience Inventory in hand, we will now discuss the development of your résumé by reviewing the primary objective of each section and where the relevant content for that section will come from. Refer to Exhibit 7.4 on page 57 for the sample Résumé Template.

Résumé Sections

Summary

Include a two- or three-sentence summary of your background, experience, and career aspirations. In many respects this can be one of the most difficult aspects of the résumé to prepare, as you want to consider your full Professional Experience Inventory and Personal Profile as you craft these sentences. Use full, complete sentences, and be as clear and concise as possible.

Note: Be sure your expectations and aspirations are in line with what your prospective employer can provide. Otherwise, you may unexpectedly disqualify yourself right from the start because the employer may feel that they will be unable to meet your expectations with the position you are applying for, and that you may ultimately become an unhappy employee.

General Qualifications

In this section, solidify your qualifications as they relate to the opportunity you are pursuing. Include and restate the three items you included in the second section of your Summary of Qualifications, and add two additional items based on information in your Professional Experience Inventory. Providing *recent* and *relevant* experiences and how they *specifically* relate to the expectations of the new opportunity is most critical.

Experience Profile

This section on a typical résumé can take a hundred different forms and be anywhere from one to five pages (or more) in length. Some people like to list every job experience they have had since childhood, while others take an overly concise approach.

I contend that it is better to include a fewer number of experiences and to provide more detail on each of them. The amount of detail should allow your reader to have a solid understanding of your work experience and reduce or eliminate unanswered questions. For the majority of hiring managers, details regarding your three most recent and relevant experiences will suffice. If you feel the need to expand your experience profile beyond that, limit the expanded (and older) items to a bulleted list that includes the company name, position, and time period.

Complete each sub-section of the Experience Profile using the same data you prepared in your Professional Experience Inventory.

Relevant Business and Technical Skills

Include in this section any experience you have with industry-specific tools or applications that the company may be using. This lets them know that there will not be a learning curve or additional education required if you are selected for a position. Complete this section using the information from the Key Skills section of your Professional Experience Inventory.

Education

Education, a section that typically does not receive enough attention, is an extremely important aspect of the résumé. It seems to always fall at the end of the résumé, even in our template version, but that doesn't make it any less important. The objective is to delineate degrees awarded, continuing education efforts, and any relevant coursework (completed or in progress). Show your prospective employer that you are continually making an effort to improve and educate yourself. Pull this information from the Personal Profile Inventory.

Résumé Preparation Challenges

As you prepare your résumé, different challenges inevitably arise. Let's take a moment to identify some of those challenges and how to overcome them.

Gaps in Work History

A gap in work history can happen for many different reasons. Maybe you took a year off to travel the globe, or maybe you were laid off from a job and it took a few months to get back to work. Maybe you took maternity leave after the birth of your child. There is really only one way to address a gap in your work history, and that is by addressing it. Submitting a résumé with a gap in work history with no explanation almost always raises a question, but more likely it raises a red flag (you don't want those). The person reviewing the résumé may think you have done something wrong that caused you to be out of work, or may think that you are hiding something. Whatever the reason for the gap, just be honest, explain it, and talk about any positive aspects of having that time off. In most cases, the interviewer will appreciate your explanation and understand.

Less Than Stellar Recent Experience

Maybe you were in a past job for a short period of time, or maybe the job didn't work out for whatever reason. In this and really in all cases, you must focus on the positive aspects of your background, and let your prospective employer use those aspects to evaluate you. You may have had a bad experience that you fear your prospective employer will find out about—through contact with your past employer, for example. Again, like with a gap in your work history, the approach is to be honest. Explain the situation, how you have learned from it, and how you plan to prevent a similar situation in the future.

Limited or No Relevant Experience

This situation arises especially for recent college graduates entering the work force, workers with a short period of work experience, and individuals wishing to make a career change. You may need to be more creative, but all you really need to do is talk about the positive experiences you did have, explain your successes and what you've learned, and try to apply that to what you believe will be expected of you in the new role.

If you are a recent college graduate, convey your solid work ethic and any history, regardless of the job, and talk about internships or individual courses completed and how that experience will be useful in your new role. Tell your prospective employer about your summer job as a camp counselor, how you worked fifty hours a week to teach young children how to swim, and how that experience, in addition to leading songs at the evening campfires, helped to develop your interpersonal skills and how those skills will prove effective for the marketing job you are applying for.

The bottom line is you have a lot of very positive personal and professionally related qualities. Focus on the best ones and share them with your prospective employer with passion, confidence, and conviction.

References Are Available (Not Upon Request)

Just about every résumé has a section at the end that says, "References Available Upon Request." Why don't people just provide them? If a hiring manager is interested in you, you will be asked to provide references. When that happens, it puts you in a reactive position and forces you to pull something together quickly—and the resulting product is usually not very good. Remember, you want to be proactive in obtaining the necessary reference information you need and in providing it to your prospective employer before he or she even needs to ask.

Provide your prospective employer with a References Summary—before you are asked for it.

Exhibit 7.5 on page 59 shows an example of a References Summary that you include in your credentials package. Because you completed your Professional Experience Inventory in the previous chapter (page 36), you have all of the information you need for this template. In preparing your References Summary, keep in mind the following:

- Include at least two *recent and relevant* business references—no personal references. As a general rule, personal references do not provide any significant benefit and can be a negative if that is all that is presented. What your prospective employer wants are references that include direct managers, customers, and other management personnel.

- Do not be afraid to write quotes (attributed to your past employers) yourself, based upon what they may have said to you, or how you think they feel about you, then ask them if you can include what you prepared as their quote on your credentials. They will appreciate you doing it for them, and will almost always agree.

- Keep your References Summary to one page.

- You absolutely need references, so prepare and include them in your credentials package *now*.

Preparing a References Summary and including it in your credentials has numerous positive benefits. Doing so saves the hiring manager from having to ask for them later. In many cases, the inclusion of quotes from a past manager will suffice, saving the hiring manager from additional calls. Most importantly, because no one else is providing references up front, you differentiate yourself again from the rest of your competition.

Exhibit 7.2
Standard Cover Letter

Month DD, YYYY

Mr. John Smith
XYZ Corporation
1234 North Shore Drive
My Town, IL 12345-6789

Dear Mr. Smith:

Through my extensive research of your company and your role in the marketplace, I feel that I am exceptionally qualified to be considered for your current open position of _____ .

I have included a Summary of Qualifications that specifically shares how my qualifications satisfy the expectations of this position and why I feel I would be an excellent addition to your organization.

I have also included detailed credentials of my most recent successes and have also provided references from my most recent employers. Finally, because personal attributes are critically important in the qualification of a person, I have included a Personal Profile reflecting all of my positive non-work qualities.

I would welcome the opportunity to meet with you to discuss my abilities further, and I look forward to meeting you.

Sincerely,

Your Name
(123) 456-7890
yourname@email.com

Exhibit 7.3
Summary of Qualifications

Summary of Qualifications
For [Your name here]

Position to be Considered For: [Insert position title here]

I feel I am an extremely qualified candidate for this position for the following reasons:
1. **I understand the expectations of the company and the position.**
   a. Statement about the company and their top one or two business goals/objectives (can be found on website or in annual report)
   b. I understand that this position entails …
      i.   General scope
      ii. Responsibilities
      iii. Requirements
         1. Primary requirement 1
         2. Primary requirement 2

2. **I have very recent and relevant experience.**
   a. I satisfy requirement 1 with my experience over the last X years at
   _____ .

   b. I satisfy requirement 2 with my experience over the last X years at
   _____ .

   c. I have the necessary (insert specific reference) experience you are looking for, bringing to the position a proven track record of successfully delivering by_____   _____ .

3. **I have personal, non-work attributes that will prove valuable to my success in this role.**
   a. #1 personal attribute and why it is relevant
   b. #2 personal attribute and why it is relevant
   c. #3 personal attribute and why it is relevant

4. **I want to be an integral part of the continued future success of XYZ Corporation.**

   [Insert your understanding of the company's mission, goals, plans, and industry outlook and how you feel you can make a difference]

I would welcome the opportunity to meet with you to discuss my credentials and how I can apply my skills and experience to this position to be a successful team member with your organization.

Exhibit 7.4
Sample Résumé Template

Your Name

SUMMARY
Include a two or three sentence overall summary of your background, experience, and career aspirations.

GENERAL QUALIFICATIONS
- Comprehensive/recent/relevant/comparable experience in the_____industry/field
- Successful realization of _____.
- Unique ability to _____.
- Excellent interpersonal skills, and the ability to communicate effectively with co-workers, management, and customers

EXPERIENCE PROFILE
Company Name #1 (Month, Year – Month, Year)
Position Title #1

Include a brief description of the position, one to two sentences in length.

Key Accomplishments:
- Accomplishment #1
- Accomplishment #2

Primary Job Responsibilities:
- Job Responsibility #1
- Job Responsibility #2

Learning and Development:
- Item #1
- Item #2

Key Skills Utilized:
- Item #1
- Item #2

** Include a full Experience Profile (as above) for each of the last three experiences you had.

Company Name #2 (Month, Year – Month, Year)
Position Title #2

Company Name #3 (Month, Year – Month, Year)
Position Title #3

RELEVANT BUSINESS AND TECHNICAL SKILLS

Proficient in the use of _____ project management tool(s),
_____ design tool(s), Microsoft Office,
_____ .

(Include in this section any industry-specific tools or applications that companies my be using to let them know that there will not be a learning curve if you are selected for a position.)

EDUCATION

Degree(s):
Name of Educational Institution, City, State
Name of Degree Awarded, Year

Continued Education Efforts:
Name of Educational Institution, City, State
Name of Program Completed (or in progress), Year

Related Coursework:
Name of Course, Actual or Planned Completion Date

Education Efforts in Progress:
Name of Program
Expected Completion Date

Exhibit 7.5
References Summary Example

References Summary

For [Your name here]

Below are recent and relevant business references that I feel can verify the experiences I have included in my credentials. Please feel free to contact them at your convenience. They will be happy to share with you my past successes and how my skills and experience are suitable for your open position.

Jane Smith
Vice President of Operations
Company 123 (123) 456-7890
jsmith@company123.com

"Jim was a refreshing alternative for us over the last two years. His personal attention to detail assured us that our project was going to be successful before it even started. He has great interpersonal skills and the ability to effectively work with and manage all levels of resources involved in a project. He is a proven leader and project manager and was instrumental in insuring that our projects were completed on time and within our project constraints.

I would certainly recommend Jim for any project manager position."

John Doe
Executive Director
Unique Services, Inc.
(321) 890-4567
jdoe@uniqueservices.com

"Jim was one of our best and brightest project managers, and was critical in helping us complete some very successful projects. Everyone loved to work with him, and he had the genuine ability to lead and manage people while implementing our corporate project management disciplines.

I would highly recommend Jim for any senior project management position where success is the only option."

CHAPTER 8

Presenting Your Credentials

You've come a long way, and you've got to be feeling pretty good about what you have prepared so far. Good work!

You have compiled a credentials package that effectively represents everything your prospective employer needs and wants to know about you. You have invested a significant amount of time and effort in the preparation of your credentials and the effort exceeds what your competition has put forth. By how much? The amount of your personal effort dictates the answer to that question, but I can tell you it can amount to 100, 200, or even 500 percent! That's what I call differentiation, and it will give you the edge to get that next great career opportunity.

Credentials Presentation Objectives

You will notice that I use the term "presentation" when I talk about getting your credentials into the hands of a prospective employer. The word typically used is "submission" or "submit." However, in my last fifteen years in the consulting business, we always used the word "presentation" instead. It was received more positively by the hiring manager because it was a little different and ended up making us do a little more than everyone else to make a good impression. Submission tends to imply simply sending a résumé to someone. Presentation warrants that you go so far as to make a great impression. It's a subtle difference, but one that has proven effective.

There are three primary objectives to accomplish with the effective presentation of your credentials.

1. *Getting it to the right person*

How many résumés are submitted to a general electronic mailbox or the "Human Resources Department" at an organization? Regardless of how you do it, you *must* send your résumé to a person, a living and breathing individual with a unique name and hopefully who has an interest in what you are sending. Your completed Job Profile should have the name of the right person you identified and who you want to make sure gets your credentials.

2. *Getting noticed*

You *must* stand out from all the rest. There is no doubt that the credentials package you prepared will be looked at favorably, for it is unlike any other. But it must be looked at, and the approach you take for presenting your credentials for consideration will facilitate that.

3. *Getting an interview*

This is the whole ball of wax. You ultimately want to get noticed by the hiring manager. You want to be impressive enough that he or she "has to meet you." Meeting the hiring manager *in person* puts the finishing touches on the manager's perception of you and allows you the opportunity to complete your evaluation of the company, the position, and the work environment. This means you want your credentials package to be considered by the person who has a direct impact on your ability to get an interview.

Presentation Challenges

Get to the right person, get noticed, and get the interview. Before we discuss how to make that happen, let's discuss some of the inherent challenges and problems with the hiring process, specifically the credential review process. These challenges are by no means insurmountable. However, they can become frustrating roadblocks that prevent you from accomplishing the objectives outlined above. Let's take a look at some of them now.

The Black Hole

You may have experienced this before. You send off your résumé to a general mailbox, electronic or physical, and it disappears. There is no feedback, no response whatsoever, and you can only sit back and wonder. *Is there anybody out there? Where did it go? Did anyone see it? What do I do now? Should I wait? Should I follow up? If so, with whom?*

That's just too much pressure, too much uncertainty, too many questions. Make sure you are never in that position again, and ensure that you send your credentials to a *specific person*, whatever it takes.

Present your credentials package to a specific person.

Electronic Filtering

When you submit your credentials electronically, there is a good possibility it will go through automated filtering, where software programs search your credentials for qualifying words or combinations of words to determine if you match the requirements of a company or a specific job. Companies have to filter in many cases just to accommodate the volume of inquiries and requests for consideration. Details of a company's specific filtering criteria are anyone's guess, and I wouldn't suggest trying to figure it out. There could be hundreds of different criteria based upon the company and the specific position, and the automated criteria of one company can be substantially different from another company you are considering.

Manual Filtering

Instead of an automated application, algorithm, or program, a real person does manual filtering. This individual has the responsibility to assess your credentials and determine if there is an appropriate match to the position. The fact that a person is looking at your credentials is a good thing; hopefully he or she will take one look and immediately put your package into the "yes" pile. Unfortunately, individuals in this position have the ability to objectively *and* subjectively assess your credentials. That assessment could differ among the many individuals involved. In this case you're also assuming that the person screening your credentials has the same understanding and expectations of the position as the hiring manager. This is a huge assumption and does not always hold true.

The Gatekeeper

Even if you do know the name of the hiring manager and are able to send your credentials to that person directly, your package probably will first stop at the desk of that manager's administrative assistant. This can become an issue if your credentials come across the assistant's desk or mailbox looking like something other than a specific response to an open position. If the manager is actively working to fill an open position, the administrative assistant will work diligently to support that effort.

Presentation Options

If you have followed the format suggestions provided earlier, you should have a collection of documents that are prepared in a professional, consistent form. If you need to address formatting concerns at this point, refer back to Chapter 7 on page 6. You should have the following separate documents, either in hard copy or in a standard electronic format:

- Cover Letter

- Summary of Qualifications

- Résumé

- References Summary

- Personal Profile

If you have electronic documents, take each of the separate documents and save them in a single electronic file. It will be easier to send and track one file and minimize the possibility that one or more of your components is lost, disregarded, or misplaced. If you have physical documents, compile them in a professional folder or report cover.

Now that you know some of the challenges associated with delivering credentials, let's discuss overcoming those challenges and making an effective presentation. You have two options in sending credentials: electronically or as a hard copy. Each has its own benefits and shortcomings.

Presenting Credentials Electronically

Most companies employ technology to support their HR efforts. As consumers, professionals, and job seekers, we embrace technology as well and attempt to use it to our advantage to facilitate our job search efforts. Sometimes we take the technology for granted, and fall into a false sense of security relative to how it may help us. Your task is to use currently available technology to *effectively* help you satisfy your career objectives.

There are several advantages and disadvantages to presenting your credentials to a prospective employer via electronic means:

Advantages

- It's fast and easy.

- It conforms to what many companies expect.

- You can use technology and email capabilities you are comfortable with.

- You can send your package anywhere, to anyone, at any time.

Disadvantages

- You cannot always confirm a successful delivery.

- Your package may not get to the appropriate destination or person (even if you specify an individual).

- With the proliferation of email, a prospective employer may not be able to effectively manage the volume of candidates.

You have several primary avenues for presenting your electronic credentials package. Whichever option you choose, it is *imperative* that whoever receives your package understands specifically who it is from and the position you wish to be considered for. Be sure that you specify this somewhere in the electronic submission process. Your electronic submission options include:

Corporate Website

Most corporations have a website that supports their HR and employment efforts. These sites typically provide current position openings and a wealth of information about the positions and the company. Unfortunately, these sites usually require you to submit your credentials through a Web-based interface or to a general email location, which can minimize your ability to differentiate yourself.

Suggestions: After identifying positions you are interested in, contact HR to obtain the name of the relevant hiring manager. You can also use the job description to determine the department that's hiring for the position, then attempt to call that department directly to find out who is responsible for the hiring. Even if you end up presenting your credentials via the website, you still need to know who to address your cover letter to and whom you are going to be interviewing with.

Direct to a Person

If you already know the person you need to send your credentials to, send that person an email and attach your single credentials document.

Suggestions: Cut and paste your cover letter content into the body of your email. If you are able, send the email with read/return notification so you can track the receipt of the email.

Job Search Databases

There are a number of Internet-based job search and employment services that allow you to post credentials directly on their website. These sites can provide exposure to a broad array of employers and job opportunities. Unfortunately, they typically require you to enter your information in a standard form and do not allow you to obtain the background information you need (Corporate Profile, Job Profile) to qualify the opportunities yourself or to differentiate yourself as you are diligently trying to do. In addition, these sites rarely, if ever, reveal information regarding the hiring manager. These sites can provide access to your next career opportunity but may make it difficult to effectively implement the suggestions outlined in this book.

Suggestions: Do your best to follow the approach outlined in preparing your background information and credentials. Use these job search database services *in conjunction with* (not instead of) the implementation of other presentation efforts.

Presenting Credentials Physically

I am a firm believer in the benefits of developing a personal relationship with a person as a means to nab that next great career opportunity. The best way to do this is through one-on-one interaction, preferably in person. The developments in electronic communications have caused us to lose that personal touch we once had. More than that, job seekers are losing a very important link to hiring managers. Take the initiative and make the effort to establish that personal touch with your prospective employer.

Not long ago, a friend asked me for job search advice. He said to me, noticeably frustrated, "I've sent out a dozen résumés, and I haven't heard back from anyone. What should I do?" My first question back to him was, "Who are you waiting to hear back from?" He ran down the list of company names. I asked him further, "Are there any specific people that you sent your résumé to?" He looked at me quizzically and then told me the variety of general email addresses and HR departments that he had sent them to. Not one specific person. That was the issue.

As we touched on earlier, you do have the option of sending your credentials electronically to a specific person. Unfortunately, that doesn't always happen. When sending a physical package of your credentials, you are more likely to *have to* send them to a particular individual—at least that is what I suggest, and even insist upon, as we proceed with this section. Send your well-prepared credentials package to a specific person, namely the hiring manager and do your best to ensure that person gets your package. There are good reasons for this. First, you won't need to worry that your credentials were lost or are in the wrong hands. Next, you'll have a specific person to follow up with later. And finally, practically no one else is doing it. Sending a hard copy of your credentials directly to the hiring manager is another way to differentiate yourself from everyone else.

Send a physical copy of your credentials directly to the hiring manager as a way to differentiate yourself from everyone else.

Like electronic presentation, there are several advantages and disadvantages to presenting your credentials to a prospective employer physically:

Advantages

- You'll be sure your credentials make it to the hiring manager.

- The hiring manager will see your credentials package exactly as you have prepared it.

- You can track your package to a specific person and can follow up effectively.

- It is a differentiator!

Disadvantages

- It takes significantly more effort than sending an email (but you're worth it!).

- Mailing and delivery options are more expensive.

- This option does not conform to electronic-only preferences of many organizations.

Here are the primary options for getting your physical credentials package into the hands of your prospective employer and hiring manager.

In-Person Delivery

This option is exactly what it implies. Go to the office location of the hiring manager and deliver it personally. Now, this requires you to get out from behind your computer and take a trip, but that's a good thing. Get out of the house and go to the place that you really want to work. If nothing else, you'll get a good feel for the travel time and a glimpse of the work environment. You will even have the opportunity to check out the local restaurants (you'll have to go out for lunch some time) and retail options close to the company location. You may have the opportunity to meet other people at the company, even if it's only the security guard.

The best-case scenario is that you may actually have the opportunity to deliver your credentials personally to the hiring manager. Go to the security desk of the building and ask if he or she can call the manager you want to speak with. If the manager is not available, ask to speak to or meet the administrative assistant. Make every effort to leave your package with either the manager or their assistant, as opposed to just leaving it at the security desk.

Direct Delivery Service

This method requires a bit less effort in that you don't have to make a special trip to the office location. Instead, you make a trip to the nearest post office or other delivery service retail outlet. Send your package to the hiring manager, with signature delivery required. You can track the package online, know exactly when it was delivered, and who signed for it. If it's not the manager, you will have the name of the assistant or some other contact to follow up with.

Presentation by a Referral

This is arguably one of the best ways to present a physical credentials package directly to the hiring manager, and while it can be handled via email as well, I feel the in-person presentation or physical delivery options are much more effective. Whenever someone I knew handed me a person's résumé saying, "I have the résumé of someone you may be interested in speaking to for your open position," I would almost always take the time to look. Usually if someone does that, I make the assumption that the person handing me the résumé is attesting to the credentials of the person, and so I usually agree. Now you have to be careful about who you ask to present your credentials. If the person giving credentials on your behalf is not well respected or positively perceived by the hiring manager, your credentials could end up in the wastebasket.

To be successful, find some positive link to the hiring manager through another person who knows you. This referral can be a fellow alumni, past employer, member of one of your networking groups, parents, friends, etc. Find that person and you'll have direct and positive contact with the hiring manager.

Tracking Your Submissions

As you send credentials to various job opportunities, diligently track those submissions and where they are in the process of getting you an interview. Don't be afraid to follow up on each submission to ensure that it reaches your desired destination. Resend packages if needed and send follow-up letters and communications when appropriate.

To accomplish this effectively, incorporate some type of tracking mechanism. Exhibit 8.1 on page 70 provides a Submission Tracking Template. Keep track of each position you are pursuing, along with the dates of the milestones as they occur. Note that the template includes a general guideline for the time periods associated with each milestone.

Exhibit 8.1

Submission Tracking Template

Company	Position	Credentials Presented	Response Received	First Follow Up	Interview Request Received	Interview	Post Interview Follow Up	Offer Received	Offer Accepted
XYZ Corp.	Marketing Rep	mm/dd/yy	mm/dd/yy	mm/dd/yy	mm/dd/yy	mm/dd/yy	mm/dd/yy	mm/dd/yy	mm/dd/yy
			within 2 weeks of presentation	within 2 weeks of presentation	within 3 weeks of presentation	within 4 weeks of presentation	various - within 1 month of interview	within 1 month of interview	within one week of offer received

CHAPTER 9

Arranging the Job Interview

You just received the call or email. You probably didn't expect a response so quickly, but it is understandable given the amount of effort you have put in so far. There is no doubt your credentials package blew them away, and they can't wait to meet you.

So now what?

At this stage in the process, it is important to step back and understand what's going to really happen. Your primary objective in the last chapter was to get the interview. Now you have that opportunity, and how you approach arranging the interview has a direct impact on the impression you make and the ultimate outcome of the interview process. It is not just a matter of scheduling an interview.

As I've mentioned before, it is critical to establish a relationship with a prospective employer, and for me I would not be able to accomplish that effectively using email. So regardless of whether I receive a phone call or an email to arrange an interview, I always attempt to respond by phone so that I can speak with a live individual, obtain as much information as possible, and get a feel for what's in store.

Don't get me wrong. I am a big fan of email, just not for anything that is important. It is just too easy, too fast—and the tendency is to cut back on the formality, type something up as quickly as possible, and send it off. That can be a recipe for disaster in the job search process, as how you write and communicate via email says a lot about your style, personality, writing skills, etc. If you absolutely must communicate with your prospective employer via email, draft your communication, save it, and come back to it later—preferably in the morning if you have the time—so that you can review before you send it off. Be professional and draft your communication as though it were the most important letter you will ever write, as it may just be.

The request to set up an interview usually comes from a specific individual at the company. It could be someone from HR, someone from the department interested in you, or it could even be from the hiring manager. The person who calls determines how you reply and what you talk about.

When you reply to your prospective employer, keep in mind the four Ws of arranging an interview: WHEN, WHERE, WHO, and WHAT. To assist you in scheduling an interview, refer to the Interview Scheduling Summary in Exhibit 9.1 on page 79. There is quite a bit of information you need to obtain, which is another reason why you want to speak with someone directly. Asking the necessary questions verbally will seem quite logical, and I think the prospective employer will be impressed by your attention to detail. If you request the same information in an email, the perception can be quite different.

Establishing the WHEN of Your Interview

When responding to your prospective employer, make every effort to be responsive, flexible, and accommodating. Remember, you *want* to meet with them, and you *want* to arrange it so that the resulting interview will be effective and successful for everyone involved.

Keep in mind the following considerations as you arrange your interview:

Be positive and enthusiastic.

There is no bigger turnoff for an employer than for them to feel that they are imposing on you or putting you out by attempting to arrange an interview. An employer can go from red-hot to ice-cold in a moment, all depending on how you communicate to arrange the interview. That's not going to be an issue for you, though, because you're going to be in the perfect frame of mind before you speak with this person. For you, it is an honor to be considered for the position, you are looking forward to meeting everyone, and you're excited about the opportunity to discuss how you can be a great addition to the team. You get the idea.

Understand the number of people's schedules that need to be coordinated.

Most job interviews include the hiring manager, the job candidate, and a variety of other people on the team or within the organization. The person with whom you are arranging the interview may be coordinating the schedules of many people—very busy people. Understand this and be a scheduling facilitator by being cordial, cooperative, and flexible in accommodating their needs.

Allow for preparation time.

Remember, you need some time to prepare for the interview. Chapter 11 (page 89) outlines activities to pursue up to a week prior to the interview. Be flexible, but also be realistic. Do not short change yourself. You need to be prepared and ready for your interview, so schedule accordingly and allow sufficient time.

Allow for travel time.

This is usually an afterthought. Once you find out the location, and while still on the phone, try to quickly assess how long it will take to get to the interview. You don't want to schedule an 8 a.m. interview if it will take you an hour to get there, and you have to drop off your child at the daycare center at 7 a.m. Don't forget to also plan for getting lost, bad traffic, car trouble, late train, etc. Allow extra time. You can always stop in a coffee shop and review answers to interview questions if you're early.

Establishing the WHERE of Your Interview

In today's fast-paced business world, we are forever trying to do things faster, better, and more efficiently. This tends to be true for the job interview as well. Regarding where your interview will be held, you may be confronted with an employer wishing to make arrangements that will be convenient for them, but could pose significant challenges for you. Resist the temptation to be overly accommodating with respect to the location of the interview. Ultimately, there is only one optimal location, and that is the job location—in person. But there are other options your prospective employer may consider as well:

The Phone Interview

Many companies use a phone interview as a means to quickly assess potential job candidates. The phone interview allows employers to screen a large number of candidates in a short period of time. Some companies do it just because it is perceived to be easier, for the interviewer and the candidate. Unfortunately, the interview becomes impersonal and distant, and it is extremely challenging for you.

- It is difficult to make a personal connection and initiate a relationship. The personal greeting, the handshake, and the "hello" while looking the interviewer in the eye are all extremely important and completely missing from the phone interview.

- Effective communication is not just verbal. It includes body language, physical presentation, and other nonverbal cues.

- Communication capabilities alone are not perfect and are not foolproof. Sound quality, volume, line availability, and a variety of distractions are all issues for the phone interview.

- Job candidates sometimes view the phone interview as not being a "real" interview, or they view it as the first round of the interview process. For these and other reasons, the interviewee does not prepare sufficiently, or saves the best for later, but later never comes. In reality, the phone interview can be the only interview that an employer may use, and you have to be prepared as if it is the only interview you will ever get.

My recommendation is this: arrange a phone interview only as a last resort, after *all* prior efforts to arrange an in-person interview have failed. There's just too much at stake.

The Videoconference Interview

This method of job interviewing is becoming more and more popular. Most computers today come with built-in Web cameras and can (somewhat) easily facilitate a videoconference. There are also numerous corporate and public videoconference facilities available to support the interviewing process.

The videoconference is a hybrid of the phone interview and the in-person interview. It includes a visual element in the interview, but the technology has many of the same shortcomings as the telephone. With this option, you risk both audio *and* visual quality, which means more things could possibly go wrong. However, if you can guarantee (is that possible?) the capabilities of the videoconference equipment you will be using, the videoconference option could be more beneficial than a phone-only interview.

As with the option of scheduling a phone interview, my recommendation is this: arrange a video conference interview only as a last resort, after *all* prior efforts to arrange an in-person interview have failed.

The In-Person Interview: Your Primary Objective

If it wasn't clear up until now, I want you to do whatever it takes to meet with your prospective employer in person for the interview. It is the only way to make a complete presentation of yourself and the only way to continue to differentiate yourself from others competing for the same opportunity.

Do whatever you can to arrange an in-person interview.

You want to meet with your prospective employer in person, initiate personal contact, and start a personal relationship, and you want them to be able to see the "real" you. There is no other way to accomplish this than to meet in person.

When confronted with the suggestion to have a phone or videoconference interview, you can use some of the following phrases to arrange an in-person appointment.

- You're close to the office location and scheduling and travel for you is not an issue.

- You would really like to show him or her some of your work (physically).

- It's no trouble; you can be there any time. Get the interviewer to agree, and you can always figure out details later.

- You are really interested in seeing the work environment and the location.

- Come up with any other reasons to pleasantly suggest that you meet in person.

Establishing the WHO of Your Interview

Aside from you and the person conducting the interview, there can be a number of other people involved in the interview process, including:

- a representative from the HR department;

- the hiring manager's manager;

- other team members; and,

- customers served by the department.

It is important that you identify each person who will be involved, along with his or her position, responsibilities, and role in the interview process, so that you can be sufficiently prepared. You would hate to go to an interview, finish up with the hiring manager, and then realize you are meeting with two other people who will talk to you about something you are not prepared for—like a technical interview on a software product you last used three years ago. While you are making arrangements to schedule the day and time of the interview, inquire as to who will be attending and what aspects of the interviewing process each attendee will be involved in.

Establishing the WHAT of Your Interview

Obviously, your prospective employer will want to talk about *you*: your prior experience, your background, your education, and so on. Even so, when scheduling the interview, it is in your best interest to attempt to determine the specific nature of the interview. As with knowing who will participate, it is equally important to have a good idea of what topics will be covered.

Questions to ask include:

- What specific topics will the interview focus on?

- Are there specific details of my experience that you are most interested in?

- Will there be a technical interview or a review of any specific skills I may have or tools I may have experience with?

- Can I bring examples of my prior work?

- Will you have had the opportunity to speak to the references I provided?

Once you have scheduled your interview, attach your completed Interview Scheduling Summary to the Job Profile you created for this position. You will refer back to both of these documents as you prepare for your interview.

The Pre-Interview Letter

Upon scheduling your interview, immediately send a letter to the person conducting the interview. The letter will accomplish the following objectives:

- Confirm the date, time, and place of the interview.

- Convey that you know and understand who will participate in the interview and the topics to be covered.

- Reiterate the differentiating additional components of your credentials package.

- Express your desire and enthusiasm about meeting with the interviewer and the team.

- Lastly, it is just a nice, common courtesy, and no one else will be sending a similar letter—it is another simple and effective differentiator to set you apart from your competition.

Complete an Interview Scheduling Summary and send a Pre-Interview Letter to the person conducting the interview.

Please refer to Exhibit 9.2 on page 80 for an example of a Pre-Interview Letter that you can use. With your interview scheduled and a good understanding of what will be involved in the interviewing process, it's time to start preparing for the interview.

Exhibit 9.1
Interview Scheduling Summary

Company Name: XYZ Company

Position Title: _____

Interview Date: _____

Interview Time: _____ Time Zone_____

Expected Duration: _____

Interview Location: _____

    Interview Method   ☐ In Person   ☐ Phone   ☐ Videoconference

    Address _____

    Building/Floor _____

    General Directions _____

    _____

    _____

    Travel Time _____

Interview Participants:

1. Name _____ Title/Role_____
Their Interest _____

2. Name _____ Title/Role_____
Their Interest _____

3. Name _____ Title/Role_____
Their Interest _____

4. Name _____ Title/Role_____
Their Interest _____

Specific Interview Topics: _____

_____

_____

_____

Exhibit 9.2
Pre-Interview Letter Template

Month DD, YYYY

Mr. John Smith
XYZ Corporation
1234 North Shore Drive
My Town, IL 12345-6789

Dear Mr. Smith:

I appreciate the opportunity to meet with you and your team for a personal interview on_____ . I am excited to meet you and am interested in speaking with you and (other interviewers) so I can better understand the responsibilities and expectations of the position.

I understand that the interview will focus on_____. Since we will be limited to discussing these topics, I wanted to remind you that there is additional documentation in my credentials package that I sent that will give you a better insight as to_____ .

I hope you found my credentials package to be complete. However, if there is any additional information I can provide to facilitate your assessment of my background, please let me know and I will provide it prior to the interview or I will bring it with me.

I look forward to meeting you.

Sincerely,

Your Name
(123) 456-7890
yourname@email.com

CHAPTER 10

Honing Your Communication Skills

The ability to communicate can be one of your greatest assets. You have the ability to communicate effectively and you regularly do so in your everyday life. When communicating, you have a style, a voice, and a presence through which you reach and touch other people. Without thinking about it or analyzing it, you're pretty good at communicating, I'm sure. However, once you get into a situation that is outside your comfort zone or that may have the slightest pressure on you, it seems all bets are off for effective and efficient communication.

That's normal. When people are comfortable, interacting with others is easy. When they're uncomfortable, nervous, or under pressure, many people have the tendency to change the way they communicate. They may freeze up, become a bit more reserved, shift eye contact, or change vocal volume or projection. They may not necessarily even recognize the change. People worry about what someone thinks, they're afraid that they will say the wrong thing, they feel intimidated. Whatever the reason, if this usually happens to you, it doesn't have to affect the way you communicate—especially when it comes to your job interview.

As you approach your job interview and all subsequent career-related interactions, your goal is to make those situations as comfortable for you as possible so you can focus your efforts on communicating effectively to get that next great career opportunity.

Three key activities of communication are *share, make known,* and *reveal.* Using these, your communication effectiveness in the interview will increase significantly. You will also find that the techniques for ensuring effective communication will prove useful in all aspects of your personal and professional life.

 In all of your interactions, focus on activities that will improve your ability to *share, make known,* and *reveal.*

Share

You have an incredible background of life and work experiences. No matter what your age, you have a wealth of unique qualities that make you special. In an interview, you have someone who really wants to know about all these qualities—wants to know all about you. *Share* your experiences and qualities with them, because they want you to.

Make Known

With all of the effort put forth in the preparation of your credentials package, you have done a fantastic job of *making known* to anyone who has looked at it and read it what a great job candidate you are. In the interview, it will be your objective to ensure (*make known*) that your interviewer remembers and understands the important aspects of your credentials.

Reveal

Finally, at the interview you have the opportunity to *reveal* what makes you special, interesting, and the perfect person for the job. You want to make these revelations through deliberate and clear actions. No amount of writing or preparing of documents can do this for you. Only in that one-on-one interview setting can you make that personal connection with the interviewer to *reveal* something additional that will intrigue and impress them. Your goal is to *reveal* to them what specifically makes you different than any other person on the planet.

Assessing Your Current Communication Skills

Everyone has a certain level of communication skills; you just need to hone in on yours. To do that, for a very short period of time prior

DAN BURNS—Author

Self-Adhesive Name Badge

Do not apply to leather, suede, velvet corduroy, vinyl, plastic or silk.

1-800-462-8379
www.avery.com

AVERY®

to your interview, focus on your communication abilities. You should identify opportunities to make small, incremental improvements in your approach so you are better prepared to make a great impression at the interview.

 Make a concentrated effort to assess and improve your communication skills prior to the interview and *practice, practice, practice.*

Most people don't give much thought to their communication abilities or their approach prior to a job interview. Whether you're really good at it or just marginal, consider your abilities for a moment. Ask yourself the following questions:

- *What are my strongest communication skills?* For any strengths you identify, make an effort to build on them and enhance them through the development of other skills.

- *What are my weakest communication skills?* Everyone has the ability to improve, especially when it comes to communication skills. Try to identify three skills to improve on, then highlight and focus on the one that will add most to your current strengths.

- *Am I comfortable looking at people directly when I speak to them?* Starting today, be conscious of this and make the effort to look at people directly in your everyday communications. We will talk more about how to practice this in the next chapter.

- *Do I find myself speaking softly when I am in an uncomfortable situation?* This is likely not something that you regularly notice. Ask your friends, family, and co-workers what they think.

- *Do I sometimes find it difficult to find the right thing to say?* Everyone struggles with this at some point. The key to overcoming this challenge is preparation. The more prepared you are for the interview, the easier you will find it to come up with the right thing to say and you will be able to say it with confidence and conviction.

- *Am I comfortable with my speaking voice in an interview or business setting?* Comfort in your voice comes with confidence, and confidence comes with being sufficiently prepared. Focus on preparing.

- *What makes me most apprehensive about the interview setting?* What's the one thing that concerns you the most? Is it meeting someone new? Is it fear of failure? The interviewer is a regular person just like you and me, and you will be more prepared than any other job candidate, so there's nothing to worry about.

- *When am I most comfortable communicating with someone? What is the setting; what are the variables that create that comfortable environment?* Identify the setting and the variables so you can focus on and attempt to re-create those variables in the interview setting. Are you more comfortable speaking with people you know and know things about? If so, what can you do prior to and during the interview to learn something about the interviewer?

- *Am I more comfortable when I am sufficiently prepared and I know what I'm talking about?* Your answer is likely yes. You know what needs to be done then.

Think about each of these questions and write down a few thoughts on each of them. Think about any other issues, concerns, or situations regarding your communication skills. You'll be surprised how easy it is to assess your own abilities, if you can set aside the time to do so. You will also realize that unless you ask yourself these questions, you won't know where you need to focus your efforts to make improvement, any kind of improvement.

What You Can Improve in 60 Days

Starting today, you have the ability to further develop your communication skills. That will continue to be the case, no matter how old or how successful you may become. Take that first step to improve before your next interview and continue to make small and incremental improvements over time.

You'd be amazed at what you could do if you set your mind to it. Haven't we all heard that before? It is true, and when it comes to communication skills, there is no doubt that you can make a substantial improvement prior to your interview. After thinking through the questions above, write down the top three communication challenges you have or the top three things you would like to improve on. Remember that everyone has the ability to improve, even if it is only slight improvement.

Your top three communication challenges might look something like this:

1. I get nervous during a job interview and that makes me uncomfortable. I wish I could prevent that.

2. I have a soft voice and I worry that the interviewer won't be able to hear me clearly, or that I will be perceived as not persuasive enough.

3. I know I'm supposed to make and keep eye contact with the person, but I tend to look down at my notes frequently during an interview.

Your list may be longer, but what is most important is that you have identified things you feel you can improve upon. Now just pick one of those items and work on it for the next 60 days, or the next thirty days, or however long it takes you to realize the desired improvement. You can work on more than one desired improvement, but even if you improve on just one of your challenges, you will have improved. You will be better prepared for your next interview.

The No. 1 Key to Effective Verbal Communication: CONFIDENCE

In addition to the one item you focused on for improvement, you should also build your confidence. The simple fact is the more confident you are, specifically in relation to your abilities, experience, and personal qualities, the more comfortable you will be talking to the interviewer about those things.

Confidence improves communication. We have all been in situations where we felt uncomfortable because we assumed that the other person we were speaking to, somehow or in some way, was superior to us. We assumed that the person was better educated, more experienced, more successful. This happens frequently in the interview setting. We assume that an interviewer, who is in a position of authority and responsibility and who we will be working for, is superior to us. Your assumptions or perceptions may very well be true. Regardless, there is only one person that is the expert on *you*. You simply need to know this fact, believe in it, and substantiate it with your interviewer. When it comes to knowing and understanding your specific experiences, skills, and personal qualities, there is no one more superior than you.

Confidence is strengthened by five main variables. By addressing each of them, you can walk into your next interview with the confidence necessary to impress the interviewer and win that next great job opportunity.

Focus on the following confidence builders.

1. Good Posture

This is an easy one. Good posture is often overlooked, and it can have a tremendous impact on how confidence is projected in an interview setting. Start improving your posture today by sitting up straight with both feet planted firmly on the floor in front of you and with your hands on your lap. Make an effort to do it at work, at the dinner table, and even when you are watching television. Eventually good posture will become habit.

2. Sharp, Professional Attire

Appropriate attire is sometimes taken for granted. Unfortunately, attire can sometimes detract from your overall communication effectiveness. If your outfit for some reason bothers you, makes you uncomfortable, or forces you to be concerned or think about it during an interview, you will not be focusing on your communication. The point is this: if, because of your outfit, you look good and feel good, then you will certainly be more confident during the interview. You will also send some great non-verbal impressions to your interviewer. (For more on dressing professionally for the interview, see Chapter 12; page 98.)

3. Knowledge

This refers to knowledge of your past experiences, your prospective employer, and the responsibilities and expectations of the new opportunity you are pursuing. Review your past experiences as you have prepared them in your credentials so that you are comfortable with those experiences. You should be able to elaborate on each of them, if needed. Review your Company Profile and Job Profile to solidify your understanding of the company and the specific job opportunity. You've done your homework; you just need to study and review prior to your interview. If you have a solid grasp of the details of your Company and Job Profiles and your credentials, no one can give you a challenge you can't handle. Knowledge will bring ironclad confidence to not only discuss these topics during an interview, but also to feel comfortable answering any questions.

4. Preparation

As I've established, you have to believe that your next interview is going to provide the opportunity you've always wanted. That means your next job interview could be one of the most important events of your life. When you get this next job, it's going to provide the financial and career benefits that you have worked so hard to achieve. Believe it and prepare accordingly. The more you prepare, the more confidence you will have and the more successful your interview will be. You may not have another chance. You are the expert on *you* and everything related to *you*. You have to believe this and believe in yourself. Prepare, practice, and walk into that interview with the confidence that you are truly the best person for the job.

5. Practice, Practice, Practice

If you want to be a great golfer, you practice. If you want to be a great musician, you practice. If you want to be a great interviewer, and impress your prospective employer to hire you, you also have to practice. Assume nothing and practice everything. Practice builds confidence and confidence facilitates effective communication.

Interview Role Playing

An invaluable way to build your confidence and prepare for your interview is to rehearse the interview. You can do this by yourself, but it is much more effective, and I think more fun, if you can do it with someone else. It can be a friend, family member, business associate, or just about anyone you are comfortable with. The only requirement is that the person must care about helping you, and you should trust the person and his or her ability to help you.

To set up a mock interview:

- Prepare a list of possible interview questions and answers. Take a trip to the bookstore or library and look at interviewing books for ideas. Include topics that you feel may be covered based upon your research and understanding of the position. Also think about questions specific to each individual you may be interviewing with, as they will all interview from a different perspective.

- Ask friends, family members, and associates about difficult questions they may have been asked in past interviews and prepare for those questions.

- Have your full credentials package available, and if possible provide it ahead of time to the person who will be participating in your mock interview.

Schedule ninety minutes to complete your role-playing exercise and approach it as though it were an actual interview. You can even dress the part in order to get feedback from your mock interviewer on how you look. Plan on 60 minutes for the interview and thirty minutes to discuss how it went, what worked well, and what you may want to work on. You may also find it helpful to record your practice interview so you can refer back to it later.

CHAPTER 11

Preparing for the Interview

If you expect to show up on the day of the interview without any prior preparation, reconsider. It is true that some people approach the interview in that way, but you're not "some people." Everything you have done up until now has differentiated your application, and the effort you put forth to prepare for the interview will be no different. Leave no stone unturned, and leave no detail unaddressed. What you do in the week before, the day before, and the morning of the interview will put you in the perfect position to make a great first impression and ultimately close the deal on your next career opportunity.

We will spend a majority of this chapter on how to prepare for the in-person interview, which is your primary objective. The activities suggested for the in-person interview can be applied to any interview format, but they are often overlooked when approaching more "convenient" interview formats. At the end of the chapter, we will review specific preparation activities for the phone and videoconference interviews.

Preparing for the Interview: T-Minus Seven Days (and Counting)

Imagine that you are a member of space shuttle mission control, working as a team with other men and women to ensure the safety of the astronaut passengers and successful launch of the shuttle. Imagine the preparation that takes place in the days and weeks prior to the launch. Imagine the individual efforts put forth, the commitment, the attention to detail—every detail having a direct and significant impact on the success of the mission. At the same time, imagine what can happen if just one detail is not addressed. Billions of dollars are at stake, as are the lives of the astronauts.

Think of the interview in the same context as preparing for a shuttle launch. *Every detail you address will have a direct impact on the success of your interview.* For every detail you do not address, there is a corresponding potential *risk* of a problem or issue arising during your interview. While there are certainly no lives at stake and the financial impact of a failed interview is not billions of dollars, there are still several reasons for you to address every detail to ensure a perfect and successful interview.

First, like a space shuttle launch, you have only one chance, and there are really only two outcomes: success and failure. You have only one chance to make a great first impression, only one chance to make a positive and lasting impression, only one chance to ace the interview and beat out your competition. Second, you have a limited number of opportunities to prepare and interview in your lifetime. You must take advantage of each interview as though it is the only opportunity you will ever have. Prepare appropriately for your interview, and your need to interview further will be reduced or even eliminated. Lastly, the interview is your opportunity to further explore the outer reaches of your capabilities and what you can and will accomplish in your career.

Complete the T-Minus Seven Days Activities for the week prior to your interview.

There is quite a bit that you need to address and prepare for in the week prior to the interview. The following is a list of the critical items.

Determine what you will wear and spruce up your image.

How you present yourself to the interviewer is extremely important. This step has a direct impact on the first impression you make and the overall success of the first 60 seconds of your interview. (We will cover this topic in more detail in Chapter 12; page 98.)

Perform a complete review of your credentials package and prepare final copies to distribute.

You have a great credentials package prepared, and you want to be sure that you have a complete understanding of everything that is in that package. Additionally, you want to be prepared to answer detailed and specific questions about anything you have provided to your prospective employer. Since some time may have passed since you initially prepared the package, spend some time to review it. Know it like the back of your hand.

In the week prior to your interview, fully review your credentials package—twice on two different occasions. On the first pass, review it to re-educate yourself or refresh your understanding. On the second pass, review your credentials from the perspective of the interviewer to identify any questions you think might be asked. Then prepare responses accordingly.

If necessary, make any final changes to your credentials package. Once you are satisfied with a final version, make enough copies for yourself and each person participating in the interview. Use a professional report cover for each of the copies of your credentials.

Complete your final practice interview activities.

Hopefully, you have already had the opportunity to complete a mock interview session (or two). Review and address the suggestions from the critique of that interview. If you have the time and can arrange it with your mock interviewer, schedule a final session to practice your approach again and address any outstanding issues. Remember: practice, practice, practice.

Review your Interview Scheduling Summary, and finalize travel arrangements and directions.

The Interview Scheduling Summary you prepared earlier has all of your interview details. Study what you have prepared and familiarize yourself with the people participating in the interview and the interview topics. You want to be able to correctly refer to each interviewer by name and understand their position in the company, their responsibilities, and what aspect of the interview they are participating in. Also, plan and finalize your travel arrangements, including method of transportation, travel schedule, detailed directions, parking options, etc.

Prepare an interview agenda, including key topics to discuss and important questions to ask.

I learned to do this early in my career when preparing to go on sales calls. When you are meeting with someone, whether for a sales call, a business meeting, or an interview, it is easy to assume that the other person (or group) has a specific agenda in mind. This is not always an appropriate assumption. What I found, and what you will find as you participate in your interviews, is that while of course they want to talk with you about your experience and the job position, there is almost never an agenda prepared, and there may or may not be time allocated to addressing all the appropriate (and most important to you) topics.

Therefore, always bring an agenda with you, as it is preferable to be prepared. Refer to Exhibit 11.1 on page 97 for a sample agenda. The agenda should address what you know or believe to be the topics your prospective employer is interested in. Be sure to include what you would like to discuss as well.

 Prepare an Interview Agenda.

An agenda is very easy to use. At the beginning of the interview, it is very reasonable to ask, "How much time do we have to talk today, and what are the specific topics you would like to cover?" If you receive a vague response, feel the interview will be unstructured, or if the interviewer asks if there are topics you would like to cover, you can easily say, "I took the liberty of preparing an agenda to guide our discussion today, if you would like to use it." Your prospective employer will be impressed by your initiative and professionalism, and you will ensure that the necessary topics are covered.

Preparing for the Interview: T-Minus One Day

If you have completed everything suggested in the week prior to your interview, there should not be anything that has not been addressed. The day before your interview should allow you the time to finalize the details of the next day's activities and make any final arrangements.

 Complete the T-Minus One Day Activities.

Confirm the interview time and location.

Call your interviewer to confirm the time and place of the interview. This will benefit you and the interviewer. In case she happened to forget or if any of the details have changed, it is better to know the day before. You can also take the opportunity to reiterate your interest in meeting to discuss your qualifications.

Set out your wardrobe and make any final wardrobe preparations.

You have your wardrobe set and ready to go (and impress). Set out everything you plan to wear and make one final inspection. Take the time to do any final ironing and one last pass of the lint brush.

Review your travel plans and mode of transportation.

Check the weather and the news for anything that might impact your travel schedule and plan accordingly. If you are driving, check the car to make sure you have enough gas and that it is in good driving condition. Check train and bus schedules to ensure there are no known changes or delays. Review your directions one final time to ensure that you are perfectly comfortable. Do not rely only on a navigation system in your car.

Get your rest!

Remember, the interview day is one of the most important days of your life. Be sure that you are well rested, alert, and ready for the challenge at hand. Go to bed at an appropriate hour to allow at least eight hours of sleep. Don't forget to set the alarm clock, and have a backup in case the alarm does not go off. Have a friend call, set a second alarm clock, or make other arrangements. You do not want to oversleep!

Preparing for the Interview: T-Minus Four Hours

This is it. The day is finally here, and you have done everything you need to put yourself in the perfect position for the day's events. You have four hours until your interview, or maybe more based upon travel time to the interview location.

I've used the four-hour window for the morning of the interview to allow sufficient time to get ready and arrive at the interview location. I also allocate time to each of the following activities, but modify them for your unique situation (to increase them, not shorten the schedule). I cannot overstress the importance of allowing enough time on the day of the interview. One of the primary reasons for an unsuccessful interview is late arrival. You can't effectively manage the first 60 seconds if you are not there for them! Plan on being early, no exceptions.

Eat a good breakfast (thirty minutes).

Hopefully, you are in the practice of eating a good breakfast every day, for it is essential. If you are not, take the opportunity on this day to treat yourself with the extra time and a good meal. Not only will a good breakfast energize you, it will also prevent you from being in the uncomfortable position of having to hide or explain a noisy, grumbling stomach.

Get yourself ready (one hour).

Today, you want everything to be perfect, so allow ample time to make yourself perfect—no shortcuts!

Get your briefcase or bag ready and complete final arrangements (thirty minutes).

Make sure you have everything you need for the day, including directions, personal identification (for security checks), copies of your credentials, and anything else you may need.

Leave for the interview on time and safely travel to the interview location (two hours).

Plan for the unexpected. Whatever you believe your travel time to be, double it. Assume there will be traffic and more of it than usual. Plan for a delay of your train or for time needed to replace a flat tire. You want to be at the interview location at least thirty minutes prior to your scheduled interview time. This will allow you sufficient time to check in with building security, use the bathroom, etc.

I still remember a funny interview situation (funny now, not then) when I was meeting an associate who was scheduled to meet with one of our clients. He called to let me know that he was running late but would make it by the scheduled meeting time. He arrived two minutes before the meeting, huffing and puffing as he hurried to meet me at the security desk. His rushing in the summer heat could be seen in his wrinkled and rumpled appearance and the perspiration dripping from his forehead. We were in big trouble. With no time to waste, I rushed him to the restroom so he could compose himself, and brushed the dandruff off his suit as he hustled away. We were lucky that day in that the client was running late, which afforded additional time for my associate to get back to normal.

Do not put yourself in that situation, as this may not be your lucky day.

Preparing for the Phone Interview

Now that you have a good feel for your preparation schedule prior to the interview, let's review some specific activities to ensure that your phone or videoconference interview is successful, if you are committed to that interview format.

If you have a phone interview, there are a few things to keep in mind to make it more effective and beneficial. Because you have completed the activities in the preceding chapters, you have made a significant impression with your credentials package. You need to manage a few other details to substantiate and maintain that impression and to minimize any negative implications arising out of the phone interview process.

- Remember time zone implications. Phone interviews allow an employer to call from anywhere, and time zone differences are the number one cause of a failed interview.

- Do not conduct a phone interview using your cell phone. You do not want to be mobile while conducting your interview, and you don't want to risk the potential quality issues that may arise. Whether you use a cell phone or not, do whatever you can to use the highest quality phone service you can get access to, and make sure the interviewer has a number for a direct line to reach you. The phone interview should take place in an area that is private, quiet, and will not allow you to be interrupted. You do not want to take an interview call at home where the doorbell will ring or family will interrupt you.

- Dress for the phone interview as you would if you were going for an in-person interview.

- If you look professional, you will feel professional, and that will come across in what you verbally communicate. Do not conduct a phone interview in your pajamas!

- Prepare for the phone interview as you would if you were going for an in-person interview.

Preparing for the Videoconference Interview

Note: All phone interview preparation activities apply to the videoconference format as well.

- Determine an appropriate location. If your web cam is connected to your desktop computer, you probably need to be where it is. With a laptop, you have a bit more flexibility. An appropriate location is one that features uninterrupted privacy, quiet, and that effectively supports your videoconference capabilities.

- Regardless of your location, be sure the view of you is appropriate. Provide a suitable and professional view of you as well as the room behind you.

- Test the communication capability and the videoconference software the day before and an hour before the actual interview.

- As with the phone interview, dress for and prepare for the videoconference interview as you would if you were going for an in-person interview. It is especially important because your interviewer will actually be able to see you.

Congratulations. All of your preparations are complete. There is one topic we will spend more time on, and that has to do with your image. In the next chapter, we'll discuss why it's so important and how to improve it.

Exhibit 11.1
Interview Agenda

Interview with Jane Smith
For the Position of _____
Month, Day, Year

Agenda

    I. Introductions
   II. Discussion of Position Requirements and Expectations
  III. Review and Discussion of Jane Smith's Relevant Experience
  IV. Review and Discussion of Jane Smith's Non-work Attributes
   V. Summary of Why Jane Smith is Appropriate for the Position
  VI. Follow Up and Next Steps
 VII. Conclusion

Additional Questions:
How do the efforts of the department impact the primary goals and objectives of the organization?

Handouts:

Jane Smith's Credentials Package:
- Cover Letter
- Summary of Qualifications
- Résumé
- References Summary
- Personal Profile

CHAPTER 12

Dressing Up Your Image

Until this point, you have created an undeniable, positive impression and image in the mind of your prospective employer. You didn't just send a résumé; you submitted an impressive credentials package that is unlike anything provided by any other job candidate and is unlike anything your prospective employer has ever seen before. You have exhibited a broad and clear understanding of the company and the position and have definitively outlined why you are the best person for the job. You have provided information about yourself that is revealing in so many ways, and your prospective employer is thinking, *I have got to meet this person!*

The whole premise of this book is that a hiring manager makes a decisive qualification about a job candidate within the first 60 seconds from the time they meet. Now the interview is set, they are just waiting to meet you, and the last preparation activity relates to image—the physical representation you put forth when you first meet the person who will interview you.

Everyone agrees that image is important, yet there are wide and diverse beliefs regarding how important a role it plays in the success of the interview. I feel that it is extremely important and the extent to which someone perfects his image, or goes to the trouble of improving it, is certainly a differentiator in the challenging and competitive business world. Your ability to present a positive first impression through your image does indeed matter. It could matter just a little, or it can be the one thing that causes an interviewer to select you over an equally qualified candidate. It's not only important for the job interview; it will have a significant impact on your entire career.

Do not leave anything to chance. Make every effort possible to improve your image prior to the interview. It's all about what the other person sees and the impact of that perception.

> Make the effort to improve and perfect your image prior to the interview.

Your Image: The Package and the Parts

You should focus on some very simple and straightforward attributes that anyone can work on and improve. It doesn't matter if you are tall or short, fat or thin, blonde hair or brown. We will focus on things that will be successful for anyone wanting to make the effort. As with other aspects of the job search, with your image you want to pay attention to detail and focus on how you can differentiate yourself from the competition.

There are basically three components of your image. When you meet someone for the first time, and they look at you, what do they see? They see your face, your hair, and your outfit. This means that your wardrobe and your overall personal grooming habits get noticed. It's that simple, so we're going to ensure you project the most impressive image possible.

Your Image Objectives and Their Impact on the First 60 Seconds

The reason you dress up your image is to substantiate the positive impression already in the mind of the interviewer. With the right professional image, you accomplish five key objectives in the first 60 seconds of your meeting.

Meet and exceed the interviewer's expectations.

Your interviewer already has a positive impression of you. Your credentials make you stand out as a unique individual: professional, confident, and successful. When your interviewer meets you, those are the qualities they expect to see. Your image must substantiate that impression and go beyond to make the interviewer say, "Wow, this candidate looks even better than I expected." Use your image to make a better overall impression than was made with your fantastic credentials package.

Make a positive first impression.

The first impression is a unique phenomenon. When we first meet someone, we always record mentally the first impression, very often subconsciously. Your professional image makes that first impression a very conscious act for your interviewer. Your goal is to elicit a positive response in the mind of the interviewer, on the order of *wow, nice, sharp, impressive,* or *very professional.*

Make a positive lasting impression.

Long after your interview, you want the interviewer to distinctly remember what you looked like and the impression you made. It can be any attribute of your image, as long as it is positive. Whether because of your perfectly tailored business suit, your manicured fingernails, or your fresh haircut or style, have something for the interviewer to remember you by and differentiate you from the other job candidates.

Show attention to detail.

There is a lot to be said about dotting your i's and crossing your t's. It suggests to other people that you care, that you are willing to put in additional effort to be better than average. Showing that you care about yourself enough to address every detail to make you look great tells your interviewer a lot about the type of worker you are going to be.

Show that you take great pride in your appearance.

We have all heard the phrase, "If you've got it, flaunt it." Well, when you're done with this chapter, and you've done everything in your power to create your positive image, you will most certainly have it. You will walk into the interview looking great and feeling great, and with the confidence that your image reflects who you are and sets you apart from everyone else. And remember, increased confidence makes you more comfortable in communicating why you are the best person for the job.

Err on the Side of Sharp

I am a graduate of the school of "better safe than sorry." In preparing for any type of business meeting or for my professional career, I've always believed it is better to be overdressed than underdressed, better to over-impress than under-impress.

It all started back when I was a fresh graduate out of college, eager to get my first job in the business world. For years I had observed how professional people dressed, and I was actually looking forward to wearing a suit and tie every day—call me weird. In the weeks prior to my first interviews, I went shopping and purchased the first two real suits I ever owned. I believed there was an expectation of appropriate business attire, and I wanted to be sure that I met that expectation.

I went out on several interviews, looking good and feeling even better. In each interview, I met with people who were professionally dressed, but I noticed that when it came to wardrobe, what was accepted varied greatly from company to company and from person to person. In most cases, I was dressed at least as well—usually better—than the person interviewing me.

After I was offered my first position, I realized within my first days of employment that professional business attire was not necessarily required throughout the organization. I had just spent three hundred bucks on two new suits (it was 1985), and it didn't seem like wearing a suit every day was necessary. Management wore professional business attire every day, but it was not required for everyone else. I figured that was just perfect for me. I had a long-term goal of getting into a management position, and I was going to dress like a manager. I liked the idea of looking professional, and it made me feel professional and perform better at my job. Not surprisingly, many people within the company believed me to be a manager, and it was not long before I was in my first managerial position.

In the twenty years that followed, I have stayed the course in trying to project the best image possible. Many of my customers and clients have only ever seen me in a suit, and if on occasion I happen to leave out the tie (which doesn't happen too often), they notice and comment. I always have felt, and still do, that it takes very little additional effort to set yourself apart from the crowd when it comes to your wardrobe and image. For me, it has always proven beneficial, and I am confident that you will find it beneficial in your career as well.

Your Wardrobe

You want to use your wardrobe as a tool to enhance your overall presentation. It may be obvious, but let me reiterate that your objective is to *enhance* your overall presentation. As easy as it is to create a positive image, it is equally easy to create a not-so-positive image. As I have suggested before, pay attention to the details, and you'll be fine.

A protest I generally hear regarding clothing is that it costs a lot of money to build a good wardrobe. I don't believe that is necessarily true. Depending on the job you eventually get, you may find that you need to spend more of your income on your wardrobe, but when we're talking about preparing for an interview or two, that does not need to be the case. Ultimately, in order to get that next great job opportunity, you need just one outstanding outfit—just one. If you are successful at managing the first 60 seconds and the 60 days prior to your interview, you need one interview to close the deal.

There are many apparel stores that tailor to the working professional, so it is quite easy to get a great outfit (or two) without breaking the bank. You need to be comfortable with the amount of money you spend, but remember that it is an investment in your future. If invested wisely, the money you spend on that perfect outfit will provide significant returns down the road.

Even if you don't spend a lot, remember it's not the cost of the clothes, it's how you wear them. Whether you plan to wear clothing that you currently have or something that you purchase, the clothes must fit right. Getting the right fit is certainly a subjective qualification, but it is a qualification that more than one person needs to make. That other person is a professional tailor. Have your clothing tailored professionally prior to your interview. Well-fitting clothes can make all the difference in the world. If you are planning to wear clothing that you already have, try the ensemble on and ensure an appropriate fit. Our waistlines have a tendency to fluctuate, and styles change over time. A good tailor can help you through those changes to get the look you want.

Your Professional Image: Key Components

For the job interview, professional business attire is required. Don't question it. You want to look as professional as possible, and you'll do it better than anyone else. In the worst-case scenario, you will be overdressed and look too good, which you actually want.

Let's go through the components of your wardrobe and highlight the things you should focus on.

The Business Suit

Style

You want a conservative suit style that stands the test of time, and allows you to get the most use out of it. New style trends can be nice but may fade quickly. Focus on the quality of the material, how it will wear over time, and how the suit feels and fits.

Color

Stick with darker colors, including dark blue and dark gray. These colors always provide a consistent and professional look, and offer the best options for matching other pieces of your wardrobe.

Fit

Have the suit tailored professionally. For the money you have or will have invested in your suit, spending the extra money to ensure a perfect fit is absolutely essential.

The Shirt or Blouse

Style

Keep it simple. More important than any material, collar, or cuff style, you need to make sure that the shirt or blouse fits you. The collar should fit your neck comfortably and allow for the top button to be buttoned without strain and the sleeves should be the appropriate length.

Color

Again, keep it simple. White is perfect for all interviewing and professional situations as long as it is in fact white. Excessive wear and laundering can easily turn your white shirt to an off-white color. A white shirt or blouse is always professional looking and provides the perfect contrast to your dark suit and the perfect backdrop for any neckwear or accessories you may select.

Neckwear

Style
Any neckwear, for example a scarf or a tie, should enhance the look of your business suit. Do not use neckwear to make a statement of any kind.

Color
Soft and conservative colors that effectively match your business suit are appropriate. Bold colors and designs are not appropriate for the job interview. Instead, select simple and muted colors and patterns.

The Shoes
Black shoes. Leather. Polished.

The Accessories
Be conservative in your selection of any accessories you may wish to add to your interviewing wardrobe. Here are a few pointers:

- One wristwatch and no more than two rings. Any more will be a distraction.

- A handkerchief for your suit coat pocket can be a nice touch, but it is typically more appropriate for other situations. Leave it out.

- Earrings, if worn, should be small and unobtrusive.

- Match your belt to your shoes—black.

- Match your handbag, briefcase, or business portfolio to your shoes—black.

    Note: The interview is no place for a backpack.

Your Hair
Make an appointment with your salon or barber. Plan your appointment in the days prior to your interview and schedule it at an appropriate time that works for you.

One important point on hair—address all of it. Any hair that may be visible to the interviewer should be addressed so as not to be a distraction to the person interviewing you.

All the Rest: Makeup, Fragrances, etc.

Facial Products

Facial products work best when used in moderation. This is most certainly a subjective issue. As with other image attributes, use products to enhance your image. I think a minimalist approach is the safest way to go, but use your own best judgment, and get a second opinion from a close friend or family member.

Fragrances

With respect to the job interview and all business situations, the best fragrance is no fragrance at all. Keep your colognes and perfumes for the weekend and instead simply focus on the fresh and clean smell from your morning shower. Fragrances can be hit or miss, and it's just not worth the risk to subject your prospective employer to a scent they do not care for.

Your Hands

While not in the direct line of sight of the interviewer, when you first meet, you will shake hands with the interviewer and your hands may be in sight during the interview. Your hands should be clean, with clean and manicured fingernails. If you have a tendency to bite your nails, make an effort to stop a week prior to your interview and get a manicure.

Everything Else

Keep it simple, and take a minimalist approach. Remember, the goal is to *enhance*, not distract from your overall image.

You have already made a positive first impression with your credentials. Now you are in the perfect position to make another positive impression when you meet your prospective employer. You're going to look great, feel great, and leave them with a lasting positive impression.

Section

The First 60 Seconds

You have confidence in yourself,
which is valuable,
if not an indispensable quality.
—*Abraham Lincoln*

There are no second acts in American lives.
—*F. Scott Fitzgerald*

Exhibit 13.1

The First 60 Seconds—Activities and Objectives

Final Prep	The "Look"	The Greeting	The Relationship

```
    |         |         |         |         |         |
    0        10        20        30        40        50        60
                            SECONDS
```

Objective:	Objective:	Objective:
Candidate: Happy, confident, and excited	For the candidate: "It is truly a pleasure to meet you."	For the candidate: Make a connection
Interviewer: Wow! Yes! And Whew!	For the interviewer: *Very polite, professional, and confident. Good interpersonal skills!*	For the interviewer: *I really like this person!*

CHAPTER 13

What You Can Accomplish in Sixty Seconds

60 Seconds Is a Very Long Time

Now the time has come for you to meet your prospective employer, and if he or she is going to make a decisive qualification in the first 60 seconds of your meeting, you want to influence that decision. You have the ability to determine the outcome of that first 60 seconds, and there is a lot to prepare.

Activities and Objectives

This section of the book focuses on those activities you want to pursue in the first 60 seconds of your meeting, along with the objectives you want to accomplish. Exhibit 13.1 summarizes those activities and objectives.

What You Will Accomplish

In just a 60-second period, you will substantiate and build upon everything you have successfully accomplished and prepared for in the prior 60-day period. For 60 seconds, you will focus on satisfying the following objectives:

- *Convey an impressive "look."* As your interviewer views you for the first time, you will strive to exceed all of his or her preconceived expectations and leave a positive, long-standing first impression.

- *Exhibit your positive interpersonal skills.* You want your interviewer to see you as the polite, professional, and confident person that you are and that he or she fully expects.

- *Make a connection.* You will attempt to make a personal connection with your interviewer, which will facilitate a comfortable, positive, and advantageous interview process.

CHAPTER 14

The Final Countdown

You Always Have More Than One Chance to Make a Great First Impression

A contradiction? Maybe, but you have taken it upon yourself to disprove that thought. By closely following the strategies in the first section of this book, you will make a substantial impression on your prospective employer through the presentation of your credentials and the coordination and scheduling of the interview. The impression will be positive, and you will be asked for an in-person interview. They will want to meet you. That's impression number one, substantiating in the mind of your prospective employer that you are their number one candidate before you even meet. The only thing left is for them to meet you in person and confirm and substantiate how great you really are. You have not yet made an impression regarding your interpersonal characteristics, and now is your chance to make your second first impression.

In this section, we will focus on solidifying the employer's decision to select you as the appropriate candidate. Remember, a hiring manager makes a decisive qualification about a job candidate within the first 60 seconds from the time they meet, so you're going to lay it all on the line. If you have done everything possible in the first section of the book, the hiring manager has already made a very positive qualification of you that no other candidate can claim. Now you'll cement that qualification with your 60-second *second* impression, after which you and the interviewer will sit down and have a nice conversation that will formally be called an interview.

We are going to focus on what to do right, and also very specifically what not to do. While this may appear to be overkill, we're talking about the most important 60 seconds of your life, and you do not want there to be *any* doubt in your mind about what is and what is not important. As we proceed through this section, things *not to do* will be labeled as strikes.

This is not a baseball game, and it is not a three-strikes-and-you're-out proposition. For the job interview, and more importantly for the first 60 seconds, you may not even be allowed one strike. Any strikes overshadow the positive impressions you have made, putting yourself at a severe disadvantage.

T-Minus Thirty Minutes: The Final Preparations

Thirty minutes—that's the amount of time you want available between arriving at your interview location and when you first meet your interviewer. Not twenty-nine minutes or anything less, but add some additional time if you can arrange it. The need for a full thirty minutes is two-fold. First, the extra time allows you to complete some final preparation activities. Second, it ensures you are at the location and ready for your interview, with plenty of time to spare.

Putting Yourself in the Appropriate Frame of Mind

Are you excited?

You certainly should be. In a few minutes you will meet your potential new employer. You have put yourself in a position unlike any other candidate being considered for the position, and the hiring manager cannot wait to meet you. Everything you have done over the last 60 days has prepared you for this moment.

For most people, what comes next is the most important 60 seconds of their career. For you, it will be a quick 60 seconds during which you will cement a positive image in the mind of the interviewer, who will most certainly make a qualitative decision to select you for the open position.

It's no big deal. The first 60 seconds of your meeting with the interviewer will go by in a flash, and you're going to be great. Keep in mind the following key points as you prepare yourself mentally for your meeting.

You're confident.

With the knowledge you have acquired about the company, the position, and the people you will be meeting with, along with all of your other preparations, you can go into your interview with complete confidence in your ability to impress your prospective employer. You have earned that confidence.

You've done everything possible to prepare, and you have done more than any other candidate to get this job.

That is really all that anyone can ask for. You have made the decision to go beyond what is normally expected of a job candidate and have gone to great lengths to differentiate yourself. You have worked hard and have achieved great results all before the interview has even started. You have covered every base. There is no one better prepared for this moment than you are.

No one is more of an expert on you than you are.

No one knows you—your background, work experience, personal qualities, and everything else about you—better than you do. You are the expert. There is no one that can challenge you on any of those topics since you know them better than anyone. With that realization, you never have to worry that you will be caught off-guard with a question you cannot answer or a topic you cannot address. The interviewer wants to know about you, and all you have to do is to share what you know.

You know more about the company than any other job candidate.

With all of the effort you have put forth in completing your background research, you are certainly more knowledgeable about the company and the position than any other job candidate. You have to believe that. In addition, you'll be surprised to find out that you may even know some things about the company that your interviewer doesn't know, and you can be sure that will be perceived positively.

Strike: Do not be late for your interview! This is a strike that you will most likely not be able to recover from. Tardiness—no matter what the excuse—will be looked at negatively. Being late for an interview tells your prospective employer that you don't care, that you are poor at managing your time, and that your time is more valuable than theirs, among other things. But the biggest issue is that if you are late, you will spend your first 60 seconds providing an explanation and the rest of your interview time fighting an uphill battle. Being late is nothing but negative, so do everything in your power to ensure that does not happen.

Your Final Thirty-Minute Objectives

In your final thirty minutes, you calmly satisfy a number of objectives.

Complete the Final Preparation Checklist in the thirty minutes prior to your interview.

Exhibit 14.1 on page 116 includes a checklist for you to run through during this time.

Let them know you have arrived.

Upon arriving at the interview location, check in immediately with building security, if applicable. Let them know who you are and who you are there to see. Tell them that you are early, and ask that they notify your interviewer fifteen minutes prior to your scheduled interview time.

Turn off your cell phone and other electronic devices.

While this should be obvious enough, I can't tell you how many times someone's cell phone rang or electronic device buzzed while in the middle of an interview. You want your interviewer to know that he or she has your full and undivided attention, and there is nothing more important than your interview—and nothing is.

> **Strike:** Do not let your phone ring or any electronic device buzz during an interview!

Make a final restroom visit.

When checking in, ask where the nearest restroom is located and go there immediately. Use the facilities even if you don't need to. Run a comb through your hair, brush your teeth, and drop a breath mint. Take the opportunity to check yourself in the mirror, inspect your wardrobe, and make sure that everything is perfect.

> **Strike:** Do not put yourself in a position to have to excuse yourself from the interview to use the restroom (unless it's an emergency).

> **Strike:** Do not let your appearance go unchecked and introduce yourself to your interviewer with breakfast on your suit coat, a coffee stain on your shirt, dandruff on your collar, something nasty hanging from your face, or any other (correctable) appearance faux pas.

Find a quiet and comfortable place to wait.

Make sure any documents you plan to distribute are easily accessible.

You have remembered to bring copies of your credentials package for each person participating in the interview. Inspect them one last time and have them easily accessible in your briefcase or folder.

Review your Interview Scheduling Summary and Interview Agenda.

Take a moment to complete a final review of what you have prepared and again familiarize yourself with the people participating in the interview and the interview topics. Remember, you will want to correctly refer to each interviewer by name and understand his or her position in the company, his or her responsibilities, and what aspect of the interview he or she will be participating in. Complete a final review of the agenda that you have prepared.

Exhibit 14.1
Final Preparation Checklist
for the Thirty Minutes Prior to Your Interview

☐   Let them know you have arrived.

☐   Turn off your cell phone and any other electronic devices.

☐   Make a final restroom visit.

☐   Find a quiet and comfortable place to wait.

☐   Make sure any documents you plan to distribute are easily accessible.

☐   Review your Interview Scheduling Summary and Interview Agenda.

☐   Turn on your visual receptors.

And Remember:

- The hiring manage cannot wait to meet you.

- You are fully confident in your experiences and abilities.

- You've done everything possible to prepare for this moment, and you have done more than any other candidate to get this job.

- You have done a fantastic job of *differentiating* yourself.

- No one is more of an expert on you than you.

- You know more about the company and the position than any other job candidate.

- You are ready. Have fun.

Turn on your visual receptors.

I think this is a really important thing to do, and most job candidates never think about it or consider it, consciously at least. While you are waiting for the interviewer, look around at your surroundings. This is the place where you will be working in a very short period of time. Identify any one of a dozen unique and interesting characteristics of the space around you— it will be these things that make for an interesting discussion with your interviewer later on. What do you see? What are the people like? What does the building, lobby, and waiting area say about the company?

The Interviewer Is Expecting You

As you sit in your quiet and comfortable place waiting to be called for your interview, take the time to remember the very positive position you have put yourself in and all the positive thoughts that are going through the mind of the person who will be interviewing you. Let's run through some of those thoughts:

I have to meet this person!

There is no question that you have made an impression on the hiring manager unlike any other candidate, and this is what the hiring manager is thinking. As a result, you were contacted for an interview. The manager has most likely told staff and associates about you and how you stand apart from all the other candidates.

This candidate is really different.

Before you have even met the interviewer, you have substantiated the following:

- You understand the company and the job position.

- You have provided a solid understanding of your personal and professional qualities, specifically relevant to the job.

- You have gone beyond the norm and have distinctly differentiated yourself through all of the pre-interview activities you have completed.

- You are very interested in working for the company.

Is this candidate too good to be true?

The hiring manager cannot wait to meet you because you are a great candidate for the position. You have already answered most, if not all, of the serious questions that an interviewer might have. The questions that remain in the mind of the interviewer might include:

- *I wonder what this person looks like?*

- *Is there anything about this candidate that would change my perception? (The answer is no!)*

- *Is this person really as good as they seem?*

- *Will this candidate accept the job offer presented?*

All but the last question will be answered for the interviewer in the first moments that you meet and will be substantiated completely throughout your interview. Afterward, the final question of whether you will accept the offer presented will be the sole issue for the hiring manager. You will let the hiring manager think about that one for a while.

You're Ready!

You are prepared and confident, you look great, and you are ready to give your best 60 seconds. Relax, take a deep breath, and have fun!

CHAPTER 15

The First Look

The First
60 Seconds

- The First Look
  The Greeting
  The Relationship

Wow! Yes! Whew!

The objective of the first look is to elicit those types of responses and solidify all of the positive impressions you have made through your 60-Day Plan. Upon that first look, you want the interviewer to be thinking:

- *Wow, this person looks even better than I had imagined.*

- *Yes, I made a great decision bringing this person in for an interview (and I think I'm going to have a new employee very soon).*

- *Whew, I may have not been absolutely sure before, but I am now: this is exactly the type of person I want on my team.*

In this chapter we cover the key aspects of your "look" in the first 60 seconds of your meeting with the interviewer, why they are important, and how to do everything in your power to ensure that you elicit these types of responses. By paying particular attention to a few specific details, you will be sure to make a great impression—before a single word is even spoken.

It is important to note that we are not talking about the first 60 seconds of your interview, but more appropriately the first 60 seconds from the time your interviewer first makes visual contact with you. There's a big difference between the two. The common belief is that everything begins when you sit down in the chair in the interviewer's office and begin talking. Nothing could be further from the truth. By the time you are seated in the interviewer's office, not only has the first 60 seconds passed (never to return), but several minutes may have passed, all during which time the interviewer is looking, listening, and making a qualitative decision about you.

It is important to remember what is going through the mind of the interviewer, and it is simply this: *the interviewer wants you to be the perfect candidate so that you can be selected for the position and so that no further interviewing is necessary.* The hiring manager wants to look at you and "see" his or her next employee. After a typical several month process where the hiring manager has completed the justification and approval process for the position, worked to advertise the position, reviewed numerous résumés, and has even completed some initial interviews, there is nothing the hiring manager wants more than to fill the position. The hiring process is costly, distracting, and time consuming. The hiring manager already thinks you're a great candidate, wants you to really be all you said you are (in your credentials package), and wants to hire you. The first in-person "look" that you provide will help the hiring manager realize all of his or her expectations.

Strike: Do not underestimate the impact of the "look" that you project.

When interviewers first look at you, they will see your face, your facial expression, your hair, and what you are wearing—probably in that order. By following the earlier chapter about image and dress (page 98), you have gone to great lengths to ensure that your hair and wardrobe are perfect. The only variable left is your facial expression. You may be thinking, *Why does my facial expression matter?* The reason is simple: one look at your expression can tell your interviewer whether he or she is going to have a good interview or not.

The Look You Are Going to Project

It can be extremely subtle, but a person's facial expression says everything about what that person is thinking and feeling. It is amazing that with just one look at someone's expression you can tell whether the person is happy or sad, excited or calm, confident or insecure. You can tell whether they are tired or refreshed, serious or flippant, interested or bored. Just one or a dozen feelings can be readily interpreted by your brain and correlated into a dozen or more different facial adjustments—to your forehead, eyebrows, eyes, nose, and mouth. What a person's facial expression is conveying can be subtle or it can be very, very obvious. Either way, your interviewer will notice your expression and make a mental note of it. You will make your expression very obvious and very positive, and you will be sure that your interviewer takes notice.

When your interviewer first looks at you, he or she is going to see (and wants to see) a person that is *happy*, *confident*, and *excited* to be there. That's it. Conveying anything else can pose subsequent challenges, the biggest being trying to explain what is really going on with you (is this person all right?). That is not something you want to address, and it is certainly not something that you want your interviewer to be thinking about.

On Being Happy

It's the day of your interview, and you have every reason to be happy. You have differentiated yourself from every other candidate. You've done everything possible to convey a positive impression of yourself in the previous 60 days. You are about to meet your potential boss or employer and learn more about the company you really want to work for. The sun did rise, you did wake, and the day is going to be a fine one. It's all good!

If that's not enough, remember this: people want to be around happy people. Everyone has his or her own problems, and no one really wants to hear yours—especially in the job interview setting. For the first 60 seconds and hopefully for the duration of the interview, leave everything else behind and be happy and enjoy yourself. It's going to be a great experience.

On Being Confident

Through your diligence in completing the activities outlined in your 60-Day Plan, you have every reason to be confident. You've worked hard and the results are evident. You know more about the company and the position than any other candidate. You know more about your experience and personal qualities than anyone. You know exactly how your experience matches the expectations of the position and you have prepared and practiced for this very moment. You look great, you feel great, and you are the person for the job.

On Being Excited

You want to be excited about meeting your potential employer. You've been waiting for this day to come, and it's finally here. When everything goes as planned, you're going to finish the day with a great meeting, a great interview, and a great understanding of your new opportunity. Your prospective employer will be even more impressed than before, and want to make you a great job offer. You know this going in, and it's going to show on your face.

How to Ensure Your Perfect Facial Expression

Conveying the appropriate facial expression is very easy to do. Some of it has to do with your physical presence and the rest has to do with what is going on in your head. Let's run through the key components of how to make sure your facial expression exactly conveys how you are feeling.

Stand Up Straight

If you are sitting as your interviewer approaches, stand up. If you are standing, make a conscious effort to stand up straight, take a deep breath, and relax.

Smile

This is arguably the most important thing for you to do. Your smile will not be fake or exaggerated, but genuine and natural. Remember, you are happy and excited to be there. A simple upturn of the corners of your mouth also helps to put you in the perfect frame of mind.

Think Only Positive Thoughts

As long as it's positive, go ahead and think about it. If your mind goes blank for the moment, just try to remember that you are going to **ACE** this first 60 seconds (and your remaining time with the interviewer):

A: I have set myself **A**part from any other candidate.

C: I'm completely **C**onfident in my abilities.

E: I've already **E**xceeded the expectations of the interviewer, and I'm prepared to do even more.

What You Will Not Be Thinking (or Doing)

In my personal experience, I have found that determining "where a job candidate's head is at" is really cut and dry. It is easily noticeable if someone is in a good mood and really looking forward to the interview. It is just as easy to determine if someone is distracted or not quite ready. Whether I was coming out of my office to meet the candidate or walking down to the security desk to escort someone into the building, the first look told me everything. Many times the candidate would be standing there, hands folded in front of them and a smile on their face, and I knew we were off to a good start. Surprisingly though, there were many times when that was not the case, and that's why I think it's so important to mention. Whether it is because the candidate doesn't care, isn't thinking about his facial expression, or doesn't feel it is important, the look projected is not positive. Let me share with you just a few examples of what I'm talking about.

There is a cell phone at the candidate's ear.

This tells me that there is something else more important than the interview. *Am I intruding on this candidate's valuable time?*

There is sweat on the candidate's brow.

This tells me that the person was probably running late and had to run across town to make the appointment on time. *How will this person manage their time as an employee?*

The candidate is looking down at the ground.

Maybe the candidate is nervous or shy. *How will this person be able to interact with my team and our customers?*

There is no smile.

The mind starts to race. *What's wrong, what's the problem? Do I really want this person on my team?*

There is disheveled hair, sloppy business attire, or inappropriate attire.

Doesn't this candidate care about how they look? What will our customers think?

Maintain Your Focus

On your first meeting, you want the interviewer to know that you respect the time he or she is taking to meet with you and that there is no place you would rather be. However, given our fast-paced and often hectic lifestyles, it's easy to be distracted. When meeting your interviewer and prospective employer, you do not want any distractions.

Strike: Thinking about anything (or doing anything) that does not have a positive correlation to the next 60 seconds.

Anything that you may be thinking about that is not related to making the best impression possible in the next 60 seconds has the potential to jeopardize everything. For the next 60 seconds, there is nothing else that is more important. It's only one minute, and you can leave everything else until after you are finished with your interview.

You can do it. For just a few seconds, focus on how great everything is and you will effectively convey that feeling to your interviewer. Then you can move on to the next objective of the first 60 seconds.

Make a positive and lasting *First 60 Seconds* impression.

CHAPTER 16

The Greeting

"It Is Truly a Pleasure to Meet You."

The greeting is your first opportunity to share with your prospective employer your individual interpersonal skills. Up until now, it is likely that all of your prior communication has been through electronic or physical means. Even if you did have the opportunity to speak with your prospective employer on the phone, this is most likely your first face-to-face meeting.

The greeting typically lasts no more than ten or twenty seconds, yet as with the "look" that you convey in the first ten seconds, there is a quite a lot that must be accomplished through your greeting. The objectives of the greeting are:

1. to let the interviewer know how pleased you are to meet them, and that there is nowhere else you would rather be; and,

2. to convey that you are polite, professional, and confident.

It is imperative that you let the interviewer know how pleased you are to meet him or her. After all, this is the person who has taken the time to review (and notice) your credentials package and has taken time out of their busy schedule to talk to you about a great career opportunity. This is the person who is going to let you solidify why you are the most appropriate candidate for the position. This person may even make you a great job offer. You better believe that you're pleased to meet this person, and if there is anyone else you would rather be meeting with at this time, then you are most certainly in the wrong place.

Through verbal and nonverbal communication, you must let your interviewer know that there is no other company you would rather work for and nowhere else you would rather be.

Approaching the greeting in this way will naturally satisfy another objective: to let the interviewer know how polite, professional, and confident you are. It may seem like a lot to accomplish in a simple greeting, but if done appropriately, you can quickly and effectively build upon the positive impressions you have already made up to this point.

Before the Greeting Happens

The interviewer is about to greet you. What do you think is going through his or her mind? If you have followed your plan closely, everything the person is thinking is extremely positive. Not only have you effectively differentiated yourself and left an excellent impression prior to today, but the interviewer has also gotten a good first look at you. Remember that through the initial look, you have left them with the impressions of Wow, Yes, and Whew! The interviewer has begun the motion of extending an arm to greet you, and there is a smile on his or her face. You have already met and most likely exceeded every expectation they may have had, and you haven't even spoken a word.

What should you do if by chance the look that you conveyed just a few seconds ago was not exactly what you had hoped it to be? Sometimes unexpected things happen and maybe that first look your interviewer got from you wasn't necessarily positive or what was expected. Don't worry about it. The time has passed and you can't get it back. The question is whether you should attempt to explain your less-than-perfect initial presentation or if you should just let it go. I would suggest that for the time being you let it go. You don't want to jeopardize making a positive greeting and taking up your precious seconds with an explanation that may not change anything. Focus on your greeting and accomplishing the objectives you set out to achieve.

The Greeting

The greeting itself is not complicated. It will be over in ten seconds or so and there are just a few things to keep in mind as you deliver that greeting.

Smile

As we talked about in the previous chapter (page 119), your smile says it all. It says to your interviewer that you're happy to be there, happy to be meeting in person, and happy about the opportunity to talk further about your next great career opportunity. Remember, it's all good—let it show.

Strike: Not smiling conveys only negative impressions to the interviewer.

Make Eye Contact

Direct eye contact has many positive effects. Doing so speaks of your ability to communicate effectively and shows that you are confident. They say that the eyes are the windows to the soul, so look directly at your interviewer and let them know how great you are.

Strike: Not making direct eye contact.

Let the Interviewer Make the First Introduction

It is your interviewer's show, and he or she is in charge. Allow your interviewer the privilege of introducing him- or herself to you first.

Extend Your Hand and Provide a Firm Handshake

A firm handshake can say a lot about a person. Your handshake conveys how you feel about yourself. A firm handshake tells the other person that you are strong, comfortable, and confident. It tells the interviewer that you have high self-esteem, that you are a winner, and that you are healthy. A firm handshake says that everything is great and positive.

Note that there is some subjectivity when it comes to firmness of the handshake and also how long you should maintain grasp of the other person's hand. Most people have done this enough to be comfortable with it, but if you're not, make a point to practice it in your mock interview sessions. As a rule of thumb, make contact, give a slight squeeze, and release after two seconds.

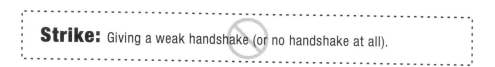

Strike: Giving a weak handshake (or no handshake at all).

Give Your Introduction and Greeting

"Mr. Smith, I'm Dan Burns. It's a pleasure to meet you."

That's all you have to say. Refer to the person directly by name and do so formally. This is not the time for referring to the interviewer by first name, even if he or she insists. It's a simple matter of professional courtesy and respect. Refer to them directly, state your name, and tell them what a pleasure it is to meet them, because it really is.

If you can squeeze it in, add: "Thank you for taking the time to meet with me."

The handshake concludes the formal greeting and introduction with the interviewer. Half of your first 60 seconds have passed, and you are continuing to impress. As you both turn to walk to an office or meeting room, there is only one thing that your interviewer is thinking: *Polite, professional, and confident—and really good interpersonal skills. I like that. We're going to have a good interview.*

CHAPTER 17

The Relationship

The First
60 Seconds
—————

√ The First Look
√ The Greeting
• The Relationship

Thirty Seconds Down, Thirty to Go

Congratulations, you're halfway there! Now you are on your way to sit down for the interview. Maybe you have just walked into the interviewer's office. Possibly you are on the elevator with your interviewer on the way to a conference room. Thirty seconds is a long time, especially when there is nothing but silence, and the person you have just met has no intention of initiating further conversation before your interview begins. You do not want dead silence, so you take the initiative to begin developing a relationship with your interviewer. In this chapter we will discuss the importance of developing a relationship, why making a connection is critical, and how to develop your initial relationship in an effective and efficient manner.

In your effort to develop a relationship in a quick thirty seconds, you want to satisfy the following objectives:

- Take the initiative and make the effort to communicate with your interviewer.

- Make a connection, and make it personal.

- Leave the interviewer with the sense of *I really like this person, and I really have a good feeling about this candidate.*

The Importance of Developing a Relationship

The jobs we work hard at and the careers we pursue occupy a good percentage of waking life. It is possible that you will spend as much or even more time with your co-workers than with your family and friends. I realize that may sound a bit depressing, but that's just the way it is. With an eight-hour workday, a couple hours of commuting time, and eight hours of sleep, that leaves just six hours for everything else. Since you'll spend that much time with your prospective employer and the people you may meet during your interview, you need to make sure that you like them. You need to be sure that you can work with these people five days a week for the foreseeable future. Work can be challenging enough without having to do it with people you dislike. Take advantage of the next thirty seconds, as well as the remainder of your meeting time, to make every effort to develop a positive relationship, at least with the person interviewing you, and hopefully with other members of the department or team as well.

The person interviewing you will have the same thought. In your case, it will be expected (hoped for with other candidates) that you are personable, friendly, and easy to get along with. You have created that expectation with everything you have done up until this point, and your prospective employer expects nothing less. Your interviewer wants to know that he or she can work with you on a professional level, but also on a personal level. Your interviewer wants to know that you can be an effective, considerate, and cooperative member of the team.

Developing a relationship is really the only thing that remains to facilitate the first 60 seconds qualitative decision that the hiring manager or interviewer will make about you. In these final thirty seconds, you start the process of developing a relationship by *making a connection* with your interviewer.

Why Making a Connection is Critical

Any relationship that you may hope to initiate and develop comes down to your ability to *make a connection* with the other person. Making a connection is based upon your ability to find commonality between you and the interviewer. Finding something in common and using that to make a connection can be accomplished in a variety of ways. Why is making a connection so important?

It's personal (and it has to be).

The primary reason you want to make a connection is because the effort—and the process—always makes it more personal, for you and the person interviewing you. You want your meeting and interview to evolve from an impersonal and business-only discussion to a warm, relaxed, and friendly discussion about your career and the people you will be working with.

It's memorable.

It's a good bet that a significant percentage of the other job candidates you are competing with will not make the additional effort to develop a personal relationship with the interviewer. Most will look forward to only the interview itself and the discussion about their résumés. Most will be looking at this day as just another interview. For you, this is something more special. This is a meeting with the person you may be working closely with as you pursue career goals, hopefully as a colleague, co-worker, and friend.

We have talked a lot about differentiation throughout this book. Making a personal connection with your interviewer is just one more way for you to differentiate yourself from your competition. Making it personal is just one more way for an interviewer to remember you. You make a connection and, as a result, they like you.

Make a personal connection with your interviewer and begin to develop a relationship.

It has a direct impact on the tone, quality, and success of the interview.

If in this short period of time you can begin to develop a relationship with the interviewer, you have the ability to change how the interview itself will unfold. Whether it is a love of traveling the world or coaching a child's baseball team, a personal connection can impact the interview in a number of very positive ways:

- The types of questions asked may change. If an interviewer really likes you, then he or she will want the interview to go smoothly and will want you to be successful. This can influence the type, quantity, and difficulty of the questions that are asked as well as the approach to asking them.

- The interviewer may put in substantially more effort to fully understand everything you are trying to get across. If he or she is willing to listen more, you will be more effective at making clear why you are the best person for the position.

- The desire to introduce you to other people on the team and within the company, and the desire to talk positively about you, increases substantially. This action on the part of the interviewer has a huge impact on your ability to get the job.

How to Make a Connection (and a Lasting Impression)

So the real question I know you are asking yourself is, "Can I accomplish all this in thirty seconds? Can I really make a connection?" The answer is yes, you can, and you will. Let's discuss some approaches for helping you succeed.

I mentioned earlier that making a connection can happen in a variety of different ways. Through this process, you want to learn about the person and show that you have a genuine interest in him or her. If you make that effort, the interviewer will most likely extend to you the same courtesy. You want to identify things you have in common with the other person—that provides the basis for your connection. For the purposes of our discussion, let's look at two broad categories of connection-making possibilities: personal (nonwork) and work related.

Discovering Personal Interests of the Interviewer

- Give the other person the opportunity to talk about him- or herself. The key is to ask specific and targeted questions (and allow the person to respond) that allow you to quickly pinpoint something that you have in common that can initiate further discussion and bonding. People naturally like to talk about themselves. All you have to do is provide the opportunity.

- Look around at the office furnishings; they say a lot about a person and can provide stimulus for a discussion.
  - pictures (family, places, pets)
  - books (personal, fiction, and business related)
  - room decorations and wall hangings
  - desk (type of worker/manager)

- Ask questions and try to relate something about yourself.
  - "I understand the company provides two weeks of vacation to employees. Do you have any travel plans coming up?"
  - "Is that a current picture of your children?"
  - "I see you like to golf (golf club in the corner). How often do you get out to play?"
  - "I can imagine you're quite busy with all of the interviewing that you are doing. What keeps you busy when you're not here at the office?"

Discovering Work-Related Attributes of the Interviewer

If you have difficulty making a connection on a personal level, initiate discussion related to the work—the company, the people, the competitors, etc. As an employee, the person you are interviewing with has interest in the company. You may find that is all the person is really interested in. You have a lot of options for generating work-related commonality.

- Again, give the other person the opportunity to talk about him- or herself or about the company or his or her position.

- Remember when you were sitting in the lobby and you turned on your visual receptors? Did you see anything interesting? Did you notice anything that could prompt a discussion?

- Try to relate current business and industry news to what you already know about the company.

- Again, ask questions:

- "I noticed the construction work in the lobby. Does the company have any other big projects planned?"

- "How long have you been with the company? When you interviewed, what sold you on the company and the position?"

- "Is this your first position with the company or have you been promoted into it?"

- "I saw that the company's stock is up sharply today. Is that because the company met its earnings goal for the quarter or is there another reason?"

It is realistic to believe that you can find something in common with just about anyone. Your job is to make a concerted effort to find that commonality and use it to make a connection. It will help you get the job, and you may end up with another good friend.

How to Not Make a Connection

While there are certainly a lot of ways to make a personal connection, there are also a number of ways to prevent a relationship from developing. You will be fine as long as you inquire about topics that reasonably fall within the realm of decency and common courtesy. Make a genuine effort to learn something about the other person. It is not an opportunity to "kiss up" and tell the person that you like his tie. You can do better than that.

I'm comfortable that you'll use your own best judgment as you talk with your interviewer. At the same time, I'll go ahead and mention a few topics that should not be discussed in the job interview setting, as the chances for a negative reaction or perception can be significantly high. These topics include:

- politics;

- religion; and,

- anything that can be construed as sexual in nature.

Strike: If you cross the line of what is appropriate to inquire or talk about in the interview setting, you run the risk of making an enemy instead of a friend. You also won't get the job. If you're unsure, don't go there.

Make the Effort

Although we have been talking about a very short period of time, just 60 seconds, a lot can happen. The impression you put forth during those first 60 seconds will most certainly be picked up on by your interviewer. As a result, a perception will be solidified, a judgment will be made, and a qualitative decision will be rendered. In your first 60 seconds, you have the opportunity to directly influence your interviewer's qualitative decision.

By making a genuine, sincere, and personal effort to develop a relationship with the person you are interviewing with, you can successfully:

- make a connection, and make it personal;

- differentiate yourself (again) from your competition;

- positively impact the interview that will follow; and,

- Leave the interviewer with the sense of *I really like and have a good feeling about this candidate.*

Make the effort to create a memorable experience for the interviewer and give the person something positive to remember you by. Also, set an additional goal to make one new friend during your interview process.

CHAPTER 18

The First 60 Seconds: Final Thoughts and Considerations

By completing the strategies in this section of the book, you have reached a significant milestone in your effort to obtain your next great career opportunity. You have provided a great "first look" to your prospective employer, a great greeting, and you have made a connection and started to develop a relationship.

Up until this point in time you have committed more time, effort, and resources to obtaining your next career opportunity than any other candidate, and the interview itself has not yet started. How great is that? You have put yourself in an enviable position, and you are sure to see the benefits of your labor as you proceed with the interview and the remainder of the hiring process. You have set the stage for the interview and have influenced it positively and in a manner that will facilitate an open, comfortable, and effective communication environment that allows you and the interviewer to get out of the interview exactly what you both want.

You should not be surprised if the interview that follows the first 60 seconds is not exactly what you thought it might be. If you have done everything right with your 60-Day Plan and have managed your first 60 seconds effectively, you may find that your one- or two-hour interview is cut back to twenty or thirty minutes. Usually a short interview means that the interviewer was not comfortable with how the interview was going and decided to cut it short. In your case, you will have already answered most of the questions your interviewer had (because he or she read through your credentials package), and there is just not as much that the interviewer needs to discuss with you. By following the strategies in the first two sections of this book, it will not be unusual for your interview to become more of a formality—more a brief opportunity for the prospective employer to meet you and confirm what they already know and believe.

Don't worry, though. In the following section we will detail the interview process, assuming that you have a full-length interview, and you will be armed with numerous techniques and strategies for effectively navigating the process and continuing to differentiate yourself in the eyes of your interviewer.

Revisiting the Phone and Videoconference Interview

I know that I have stressed the importance of the face-to-face interview and all the reasons why I want you to do everything possible to make sure that happens. However, I also realize that ultimately it is the prospective employer who makes the final decision on the interview format, and there may arise a situation where you will not be able to meet the interviewer in person.

The rules don't change just because you cannot meet with your interviewer face to face. If you must submit to a phone or videoconference interview, it is still your responsibility to be successful in accomplishing the objectives of the first 60 seconds of your meeting with your prospective employer as outlined in Chapters 13–17.

A phone or videoconference interview does not *eliminate the first 60 seconds, the critical importance of the first 60 seconds, or the decisive qualification an interviewer will make during the first 60 seconds.*

The first 60 seconds, as we are approaching it, is eliminated only if you allow it to be eliminated, and you do not want to let that happen. While it may take some additional effort on your part, you must ensure you can take advantage of the first 60 seconds of your meeting,—regardless of the interview format.

Note: Be sure to review Chapter 11 (page 89), specifically regarding the details of the phone and videoconference interview.

If you are participating in a phone or videoconference interview, you must still accomplish the following, the same as if you were there in person:

- Conduct final preparations, including the Final Preparations Checklist (Chapter 14; page 111).

- While you cannot convey it through your first look, you can, through your vocal presentation, let your interviewer know that you are happy, confident, and excited to be speaking with them. Also, your physical and mental preparations should be *exactly the same* as though you were meeting at the employer's office (Chapter 15; page 119).

- Make an effective greeting, prepare for it appropriately, and let the person know you are polite, professional, and confident (Chapter 16; page 125).

- Develop a relationship with the person and make a personal connection (Chapter 17; page 129).

All of these objectives must be realized in the phone or videoconference interview setting.

Where the Challenges Arise

There are certainly some distinct situations, issues, and challenges presented with these off-site or remote interview formats. It is best to review and understand these challenges and then work to implement some additional strategies to minimize the negative impact that may result if left unattended. Here are the primary challenges of the off-site or remote interview:

Your interviewer cannot see you in a phone interview and will be challenged to see you in a videoconference format.

What you can do:

- Consider providing a professional photograph of yourself prior to the interview. Follow the instructions on image and dress in Chapter 12 (page 98), and have someone take a digital picture. Provide a physical copy (preferred) or send one electronically.

- Let the person know you have gone to the same great lengths to prepare for the interview.

You will not be exposed to the employer's building or work environment.
What you can do:

- Visit the building prior to the interview, the same as if you were going there for the interview. In this case, you may actually have more time to look around, observe, and speak to people. Let your interviewer know that you made the effort to visit. You'll also have other topics to talk about as a result.

- Contact the HR department or someone who works at the employer's location. Explain that you are interviewing with the company and are really interested in making a great first impression, but that you are participating in an interview from a remote location. Ask him or her to describe the work environment for you.

You cannot effectively provide your "first look."
What you can do:

- Provide the details of a professional reference (from your References Summary) at the start of the interview to substantiate your professionalism, confidence, interpersonal skills, etc. If done right, you can still elicit the responses of *Wow*, *Yes*, and *Whew* from your interviewer.

- Prepare yourself mentally the same as if you were there in person. Remember, there is no one else who you would rather be speaking to at this time. You want your "first look" to come across in your voice.

You cannot shake their hand as you greet them, let them see your smile, or make direct eye contact.
What you can do:

- Tell the person that you are happy to be speaking with them.

- Verbalize the same greeting as you would if you were standing right in front of them.

You will not be able to use visual cues to make your personal connection.
What you can do:

- Instead of visual cues, you will have to listen carefully for verbal cues. This is far more difficult, but listen closely to how the interviewer speaks (volume, tone, diction, accentuation, etc.), and what he or she talks about for hints about the type of person he or she is and how your responses are being perceived.

- If there is time available, you can still ask inquiring questions to find some common ground.

You Must Do Something

These are just a few possible suggestions for you to consider as you approach the remote interview. Take the time to think about it yourself and come up with some of your own. The important point to remember is that you must do something—anything—to compensate for the inherent deficiencies of the phone or videoconference interview format. If you do, you can manage the first 60 seconds just as effectively as if you had an in-person interview, and will most certainly differentiate yourself. If you don't, you will be putting yourself at a distinct disadvantage, which would be a shame after all of the effort you have put forth.

That's it. Your first 60 seconds has passed, never to return. The time is gone, and you have done everything you could to make a positive first (or second?) impression. Whether it went perfectly or not exactly as you had hoped, you can no longer think about it or worry about it. It's time to move on to the interview with confidence and conviction, because in the back of your mind, you will know that you have accomplished a lot already. Let's take a moment to look at Exhibit 18.1 and review what you have indeed accomplished.

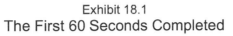

Exhibit 18.1
The First 60 Seconds Completed

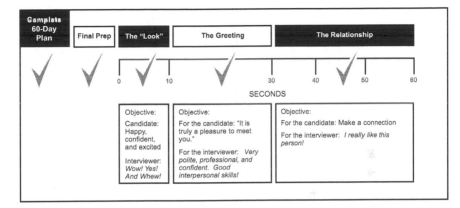

Wow! That's quite an accomplishment, and remember, the interview hasn't even started yet!

Section 3

Managing the Next 60 Minutes

Dost thou love life? Then do not squander time;
for that's the stuff life is made of.
—*Benjamin Franklin*

Lives of great men all remind us
We can make our lives sublime.
And, departing, leave behind us
Footprints on the sands of time.
—*Henry Wadsworth Longfellow*

CHAPTER 19

Setting the Stage for the Interview

As we focus on managing the next 60 minutes of your interview, you will be confronted with one of two likely scenarios. If you have been diligent in your execution of the 60-Day Plan from Section I and have effectively managed the first 60 seconds as suggested in Section II, then you are in a most enviable position. More than likely, to a great extent the decision has already been made to select you for the position and the remaining time that your interviewer spends with you is only necessary to substantiate further how he or she already feels about you. The other possibility (although unlikely if you have read this book, yet very likely for your competition) is that you are counting on the interview, and the interview alone, to convince your interviewer that you are the best person for the job. If you don't make a positive impression prior to the interview or during the first 60 seconds of your meeting, then you will be fighting an uphill battle.

Regardless of your individual situation, the interview itself is still an important part of the overall interviewing and selection process. Whether you plan to use the next 60 minutes to close the deal or make your initial pitch, there are critical objectives to satisfy during the interview process:

- Set the agenda.

- Effectively use your credentials package.

- Satisfy the expectations of the interviewer.

- Satisfy your individual expectations.

- Substantiate that they want you.

- Eliminate all obstacles.

Set the Agenda

As you begin the interview, first establish the framework for how the process (the next 60 minutes) will unfold. Each interviewer will be different, and each will have his or her own unique method of interviewing and assessing your abilities. Every interviewer will likely cover the main topics of the available position and your experience. Beyond that, other topics and time spent on each topic can vary greatly from one interviewer to the next.

Interviewers follow any one of a dozen different interview formats. The approach interviewers decide on may depend on how their day is going, how prepared they are, how much time they have available (based upon changes to their schedule as of that day), their current mood, or what they may be required to do per the guidelines of the company. A major factor impacting the interview format is any preconceived notion they may have of you, which should play a big part in your case.

The interview format that an interviewer uses has a direct impact on the resulting agenda that you want to try to suggest. It is important that you not only satisfy what the interviewer is trying to accomplish, but also satisfy your own individual objectives. By quickly understanding the interviewer's intentions, you can make your suggestions accordingly. The most popular interview formats include:

The "Tell Me About Yourself" Interview

This is a very popular interview format because it requires very little preparation time for the interviewer, who essentially puts the responsibility on you to prove to him or her that you are the appropriate person for the position. That's perfect, since this format allows you to take advantage of all your prior preparations to sell yourself.

The "Let Me Tell You about Us (and Me)" Interview

This is also a very popular option because it gives the interviewer the opportunity to share with you (or prove to you) what he or she knows about the company, department, and position. On the one hand, this format is beneficial in that it allows you to obtain much of the information you want to know about the company and the position so you can make a well-informed decision. On the other hand, you may find that very little time is left to convey all the reasons why you are the best person for the job.

The Résumé Review Interview

In this case the interviewer uses the résumé itself as the basis for all discussion, starting at the top, reading each section, and asking questions or prompting discussion accordingly. This is a good option as long as you have prepared your credentials package as recommended. Then this format allows you to walk through the package and cover all the key information points you prepared.

The Test Interview

This interview format is a popular option for the individual interested in an objective (yet sometimes limited) and quantitative assessment of your skills via a variety of tests (technical, personality, etc.). Having completed the pre-interview activities in your 60-Day Plan (as covered in Chapter 9; page 71), you should know exactly what you will be tested on and be prepared accordingly. Remember, when arranging the interview, you asked specifically about any tests that you need to take. Even if you know about the tests and have prepared sufficiently, your challenge will be to cover the other topics necessary for your interviewer to select you, as testing alone is never sufficient.

The Firing Squad Interview

This is essentially a group interview format where a variety of individuals representing various areas of a company or specific department come together to assess your abilities relative to their particular area of interest. They are usually lined up around you and take turns asking specific questions of interest to them. This interview format can be very challenging and even intimidating for some people, especially when you did not know all these people would be attending and you are not prepared. In your 60-Day Plan, hopefully you were made aware of all the participants and you have planned accordingly. You have copies of your credentials package for each participant, and you have prepared yourself to address their specific questions. If you are caught off-guard or not prepared to address the participants, your approach of setting the agenda is extremely important.

While these examples cover the main types of interview formats, there can be dozens more. Remember this: it is your responsibility—and yours only—to ensure that the interview is conducted to meet the interviewer's expectations, and yours, and is done in a way that effectively uses the time you have together. The best way to do this is by defining an agenda for your meeting at the start.

As you recall from Chapter 11 (page 89), as part of your 60-Day Plan you prepared an Interview Agenda. With this in hand, it's easy to put into use. At the beginning of the interview, it is very reasonable to ask, "How much time do we have to talk today, and what are the specific topics you would like to cover?" If the response is vague, if you feel the interview will be very unstructured, or if the interviewer asks if there are topics you would like to cover, you can easily say, "I took the liberty of preparing an agenda to guide our discussion today, and I think it covers what we are both interested in covering." You can even amend your agenda on the fly based upon your interviewer's commented expectations. Your prospective employer will be impressed by your initiative and professionalism, and you will ensure that the necessary topics are covered.

You can just as easily agree to follow an agenda that your interviewer may suggest. Use your best judgment. Either way, remember not only to include the topics that you and your interviewer want to cover, but also attempt to clarify the expectations of the interviewer (what each of you wants to accomplish), along with the time to be spent on each topic.

To summarize the objectives of setting the interview agenda:

• Confirm topics of discussion.

• Clarify expectations and objectives.

- Specify time to be spent on each topic (this is especially critical to ensure that all agenda topics are covered).

Effectively Use Your Credentials Package

Through your individual 60-Day Plan, you invested a substantial amount of time and effort in the preparation of your credentials package. Your prospective employer has received the package and because of it, you now have the opportunity to meet with them in person.

With respect to the interview, you cannot assume that your interviewer has committed your credentials package to memory, nor can you assume that the interviewer has it available at the time of your interview. It is likely that your interviewer has reviewed your credentials and that certain parts of it stood out. *You do need to assume* that you will use interview time to more fully explore and discuss what you have prepared. All the hard work is done. You have prepared a great package and as long as you have brought enough copies for all participants, you can easily refer to it throughout the agenda.

Remember that *everything* in your credentials package is available for you to use during the interview process. You can assume that your credentials package is unlike that of any other candidate, and you want to take the opportunity to make that point very clear. With it available during the interview, you and your interviewer will find it very easy (and effective) to refer to the package as you cover various topics.

Exhibit 19.1 shows all of the documents that can be used during the interview, along with a reference to the subsequent chapters that go into greater detail on how to use those documents most effectively. Have the documents available for your interview and plan to use them to *differentiate yourself* and impress your interviewer.

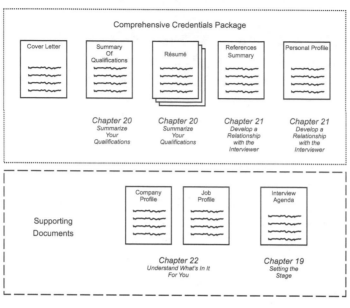

Exhibit 19.1
Referencing Your Prepared Documentation

Effectively utilize your Credentials Package during the interview.

Satisfy the Expectations of the Interviewer

This objective may be obvious, but there are ways to accomplish this most effectively, which we discuss throughout the chapters of this section. For now, focus on the following points, as they will be helpful for you throughout the interview process.

Summarize Your Qualifications

Throughout the interview, continually summarize and share your individual qualifications, *specifically as they relate to your understanding of the position.* Be clear, concise, and reference what you believe to be the expectations of the interviewer. Then provide a brief summary of the exact experiences you have that meet those expectations. Remember that your qualifications should include professional *and* personal aspects.

Effectively Respond to Questions

Regardless of your qualifications, how you respond to questions is extremely important. Your ability to be direct, clear, concise, and complete will help you satisfy the expectations of the interviewer. A few suggestions to consider:

Listen

While trying to keep direct eye contact, make a concerted effort to listen carefully to the question posed, but also feel free to take notes as the question is being asked (most people don't). Your objective is to understand exactly what your interviewer is asking and refer back to the question later if necessary. Only then will you be able to provide an appropriate response.

Confirm and Clarify

Once the question is asked, take the time to confirm and clarify your understanding of the question. I wouldn't suggest doing this for all questions, as that would be awkward (and annoying), and you will find that many questions do not require further clarification. But with a challenging question, confirming and clarifying not only ensures you will be answering the right question, it also provides you time to prepare your response. For example, if your interviewer were to say, "Tell me all about your past experience," which is a very broad question, you might respond with, "Would it be appropriate for me to start with my most recent experience and then go back to explain what I have accomplished over the last five years?"

Think

Take the time to think about what's asked and what your answer will be. Many people are uncomfortable pausing between the question and answer because it creates silence; instead they react and start talking immediately. Certainly an extended pause can be uncomfortable and can be a cause for concern by the interviewer, but you have a second or two to think about your reply. It's okay—take your time, and remember that a little silence is reasonable.

Respond

Be clear, concise, and complete, yet err on the side of brevity. Once you have provided your answer, you can always then ask, "Did that answer your question appropriately?" If your interviewer wants a further response, he or she will ask for it. Make a point to provide examples to strengthen each of your responses. Finally, you should always be honest. If you do not have an answer or are unsure about how to respond, it is acceptable to say, "I don't know, but this is how I would approach addressing that particular situation on the job."

Substantiate That They Want You and Confirm You Are the Best Candidate

Help your interviewer. You have already made a great impression and are a front-runner for the position. Continue to share your confidence and conviction (not cockiness or obnoxiousness) about why you feel your skills and experience perfectly match what your interviewer is looking for.

Eliminate All Obstacles to Employment

Your interviewer wants to hire you, wants you to be "the one." At this stage in the process, the only obstacles that may arise will be obstacles that you bring to light during the interview. *Resist the temptation to do this!* Let me explain further.

I can't tell you how many times I was in an interview where everything was going smoothly and my mind was made up to select a candidate, only to have the candidate say something to completely change my mind—in a matter of seconds! These candidates may have thought their statements were acceptable because they were telling the truth, but in reality they had a huge impact during the interviewing process. Here are some of the more popular comments I've heard before that raise a red flag for the interviewer:

- "I have to give my current employer four (or longer) weeks notice."

- "I won't be able to start a new job for two months so I can get my bonus."

- "I have a vacation (or vacations) planned that's coming up."

- "Will you be able to meet my salary expectations?"

- "I have two other companies that I'm really more interested in working for."

Each of these statements is fairly reasonable, yet in the wrong context they can be detrimental. What I want you to seriously consider is this: everything you do and say in the interview is in an effort to get your prospective employer to select you for the position *and offer you a job*. Do not do anything that may prevent your prospective employer from hiring you. The one thing you will be sure to let your interviewer know is: "I'm available!" Once you get the job offer, address your issues. We'll talk more about this in Chapter 23 (page 179).

Satisfy Your Individual Expectations

The interview is as much for your benefit as it is for the interviewer. If you play your cards right and win over the interviewer before the interview even begins (your ultimate goal), then you can use the interview time to discuss those topics and questions of most interest to you. That's probably the greatest secondary benefit of effectively implementing *The First 60 Seconds* approach. Since many of your interviewer's questions will have already been addressed, you get the opportunity to make it *your* interview. Take advantage of the time you have during the interview to get what you want out of it.

While the interviewer is ultimately interested in what is in it for them, namely how you would satisfy the responsibilities and expectations of the position, you ultimately need to understand what is in it for you. As you and the interviewer lay out the agenda for the interview, be sure to include those topics you feel are necessary to allow you to make a reasonable assessment about the opportunity and your prospective employer.

Addressing the Biggest Interviewing Challenges

There are many challenges that may arise during the interview process. The interviewer may have certain questions or concerns for you to address. There may even be issues regarding your credentials that you are aware of (even though you may deny their existence), that if not addressed appropriately, will negatively impact your chances. When you are caught off guard, the questions asked can be extremely difficult to respond to in a timely and effective manner. Conversely, if you know the issue questions that will be raised, and can prepare for them accordingly, you will be in a much better position. Below are some of the most common questions in the interview, and the corresponding chapter where we'll discuss them:

- Do you have enough experience for the position available? (Chapter 20; page 155)

- Can you explain this gap in your work experience? (Chapter 20; page 155)

- What are you really like? (Chapter 21; page 166)

- Are you interested in the position (and why)? (Chapters 22–23; pages 172 and 179)

- Will you "fit" into the work environment? (Chapter 21; page 166)

- Why did your last employment opportunity end and what have you been doing since that time? (Chapters 20–21; pages 155 and 166)

Summarize Your Qualifications

What you will need:

The entire job search and career management process comes down to an innate ability to continually sell yourself and your experience, qualifications, and abilities. You may not like to do it, but you do have the ability, and it is expected. That's just the way it is. If you do not take responsibility for helping others better understand *you*, then you're left with the assumption that the other person will make the effort to learn about you. You also have to accept the other person's interpretation of you—good or bad. Sometimes you will be fortunate to work with that special person who has the uncanny ability to somehow instinctively know all of your strengths. Unfortunately, that person comes along infrequently. A better option is to ensure that you are in control of how others perceive you and what they say about you. When it comes to your career, there's no place for assumptions. You must take initiative to make things happen.

It's easy for us to think that our colleagues and bosses should know how good we are: our extensive experience, accomplishments, and how proficient and effective we are at meeting and exceeding our job responsibilities. In my years of experience, I frequently heard statements like the following from co-workers, clients, business associates, and friends (and sometimes, early on, even from me):

- "I can't believe that person was promoted before me—I've done so much more for the company."

- "Can't the person see from my résumé how good I am? It's all right there on the page."

- "If my manager doesn't respect me for all of my years of service, then it's time for me to start looking."

You are not going to make these statements, and when it comes to your interview, you are going to be sure that you make it *perfectly clear* to your interviewer that you are the appropriate candidate for the position.

Let's assume that for your interview you will use the Interview Agenda you prepared as part of your 60-Day Plan. The two topics and objectives we discuss in this chapter are:

- discussion of position requirements and expectations; and,

- review and discussion of relevant experience and summary of why you are appropriate for the position.

In addition, we will discuss how to effectively address some of the more common challenges that may arise as you cover those agenda topics.

Discussion of Position Requirements and Expectations

At the start of an interview, it is always best to first understand the position requirements and the expectations of the manager, the company, and the specific department you will be working for. Only then can you realistically attempt to relate your relevant experience and why you are the best person for the position. If the interviewer starts with a direct question like, "Tell me about your past experience," and you do not have a prior understanding of expectations, you can't be sure that your response will provide the information your interviewer really needs to hear.

When confronted with this situation, try making the following suggestion: "I want to effectively share with you all of my relevant experience and qualifications. Could we take a moment to review the details of the position and make sure I fully understand your expectations?"

Most interviewers will gladly welcome the suggestion, as they really don't want to waste their time with irrelevant and misguided responses. If you have prepared your Company and Job Profiles, and the corresponding Summary of Qualifications as suggested in Section I, it will be very easy for you to clarify details of the position. At the same time, your interviewer will know that you have a sound understanding of the position.

Let's take a look at the Summary of Qualifications Template again (see page 158) and highlight some of the primary ways you can use this information in your discussion.

You can direct your interviewer to your prepared Summary of Qualifications. You can then discuss the following questions.

Clarify Responsibilities

"As you can see in Section 1 of my Summary of Qualifications, I've listed what I understand to be the primary responsibilities of this position. Are there other responsibilities that you feel are critical for the person in this role to possess in order to be successful?"

Clarify Position Requirements

"Based upon the job description I obtained, it's clear that the primary skill and experience requirements are a) ____, b)____, and c)____. Of those, which do you feel are the most critical, or how would you prioritize them?"

Understand Expectations

"Aside from the job responsibilities and the skills required to satisfy them, are there any other expectations you will have of me—if I am chosen—that will allow me to make you and the department be more successful?"

You are trying to accomplish a few things by asking these questions. First, they reiterate your effort to really understand the position, both before the interview and during it. Second, you want to be very clear on what the interviewer is looking for and how current expectations might differ from yours.

Exhibit 20.1
Summary of Qualifications Template

Summary of Qualifications

[Your name here]

Position to be Considered For: [Insert position title here]

I feel I am an extremely qualified candidate for this position for the following reasons:

1. **I Understand the Expectations of the Company and the Position**
   a. Statement about the company and their top one or two business goals/objectives (can be found on web site or in annual report)
   b. I understand that this position entails...
      i. General scope
      ii. Responsibilities
      iii. Requirements
         1. Primary requirement 1
         2. Primary requirement 2

2. **I have very recent and relevant experience**
   a. I satisfy requirement 1 with my experience over the last X years at _____.

   b. I satisfy requirement 2 with my experience over the last X years at _____.

   c. I have the necessary [insert specific reference) experience you are looking for, bringing to the position a proven track record of successfully delivering by_____.

3. **I have personal, nonwork attributes that will prove valuable to my success in this role**
   a. #1 personal attribute and why it is relevant
   b. #2 personal attribute and why it is relevant
   c. #3 personal attribute and why it is relevant

4. **I want to be an integral part of the continued future success of XYZ Corporation.**
   (insert your understanding of the company's mission, goals, plans, and industry outlook)

I would welcome the opportunity to meet with you to discuss my credentials and how 1 can apply them to this position to be a successful team member with your organization.

You also create the opportunity to present yourself in the most positive light. If you know exactly what the person expects, you can tailor how you present your skills and experience to those expectations. Plus, you customize your Summary of Qualifications personally to the interviewer's *current* wants and needs, which are fresh in their mind since they just shared them with you. You can tell interviewers things about yourself that satisfy their individual expectations *exactly*.

If you want to be successful in the interview, you really have only this one option. If you do not raise the necessary questions and understand what the interviewer is thinking today (because his or her expectations can certainly change from day to day), you will never know if you're on the mark with your presentation.

As an example, imagine a scenario where you jump right in and talk about your most recent experience with Software Product A—the most cutting-edge product on the market and the one you assume the employer wants you to know about, only to find out that this company is really interested in someone experienced with Software Product B (which they just converted to). Or maybe they are still using Product A, but out of the five expectations the interviewer has, it is of the least importance.

It is in your best interest to take a few moments to clarify your understanding of what your interviewer is really looking for. Even if you do not have your Summary of Qualifications in front of you, you still have the opportunity to pose intelligent and information-producing questions. Then you can move forward and effectively share your recent and relevant skills and experience with your interviewer.

Review of Relevant Experience and Why You Fit the Position

Given your fresh understanding of the responsibilities, requirements, and expectations of the position, the next step is to review and discuss your recent and relevant professional and personal experiences, educational background, and other positive qualities.

Summarize, summarize, summarize. Although you have your Summary of Qualifications and your résumé available at the interview, stick with your Summary of Qualifications to convey how your skills and experience match the expectations of the position. Think about it: the only question that your interviewer needs to have answered is: "How do your past experience and current skills match with the requirements and expectations of the position?"

As we discussed earlier, it is typically very difficult to answer this question through the résumé alone. Even if you have followed the recommended résumé format in this book, by definition and design, the résumé presents the following challenges:

- The résumé contains a lot of information, with a broad time period and scope, and is typically focused on professional experience only.

- Too much is left to subjective interpretation.

- Some information may be more relevant than other information, with the not-as-relevant content potentially confusing or overshadowing what is most relevant.

Therefore, use your Summary of Qualifications, as it not only directly answers the interviewer's "one question," but it also answers the questions of how your personal and nonwork attributes come into play (very important), and also why you personally feel you are the best person for the job (very, very important). You can suggest that you would like to start with a brief review of this document because you feel it will best answer why you are the right person for the job. If necessary, periodically refer to the résumé to strengthen a point. Additionally, after your summary, ask if the interviewer has any specific questions regarding your résumé that might require further discussion or clarification. With your Summary of Qualifications, you have done a great job helping your interviewer understand who you are, and have saved them the time and difficulty of assessing your résumé. *The interviewer will appreciate this.*

Addressing Challenges That May Arise

If you understand the position and effectively present your credentials, there should be no outstanding issues. You will have matched your personal and professional experience and qualifications specifically to the needs of the position. However, there may never be a perfect match, and when it comes to the review of your résumé, questions may arise. At some point in your career, if not already, you will be presented with numerous challenges that relate to your prior experience.

Such challenges become issues only if you allow it—if you pretend that they do not exist and do not prepare to address them. Since everything in *The First 60 Seconds* method focuses on *being proactive* and *differentiating yourself* from your competition, you need to think about these potential challenges. Address them prior to your interview with the same diligence and thoroughness as your 60-Day Plan.

Address interviewing challenges that may arise—before they arise.

You can expect that a prospective employer will have questions about you, your background, and your experience. Some questions will be easier to address than others. If there are issues with your credentials, you certainly know about them, for they are in fact your credentials. Your best approach to addressing any difficult questions is proactively, and thoroughly, before the interview even takes place. However, if you are presented with such a situation in an interview, remember to be honest, explain the situation thoroughly, and stress the positive aspects of the situation.

Let's discuss challenges that can arise and how to approach them.

Lack of or Mismatched Experience

You will never have the perfect and exact experience and qualifications that a particular position may require. Hiring managers are realistic and understand this, and while their hope is to satisfy as many of their expectations as possible, they also can be made more comfortable with an honest and realistic explanation from you regarding where there might be deficiencies. It is common for an interviewer to state, "I see from your credentials that you don't have any experience with..." If you find you do not have a particular skill or experience level that may be expected, here's what you can do:

- Be honest, and agree with the interviewer's understanding. "While it's true that I do not have that specific experience..."

- Immediately follow up with your strengths in the other areas required. "I am comfortable that my experience with _____ and my skills in the following areas will allow me to be very successful in this position."

- Share a similar experience where a past job or project required a skill you did not have and explain how you overcame that challenge. If there is a particular reference to your résumé that would be helpful, suggest it.

- Share how you plan to overcome that challenge when you are selected for the position.

- Share your personal determination to continually learn and develop, both personally and professionally. (We'll cover this in more detail in Chapter 30; page 258.)

The primary point is that *you can overcome any challenge* presented to you in an interview. You have no other choice if you are determined to be hired. Be confident and express with conviction how you will overcome any deficiency with respect to your credentials.

Gaps in Work Experience

The perfect scenario for a person reviewing a candidate's credentials is to see a continuous and uninterrupted work history. For many hiring managers, any gap of more than a few weeks between jobs can be a red flag. Many things race through the mind of the interviewer, and they're usually all negative. Some examples include:

- *Why was this person out of work so long?*

- *Good workers are always working. Is there an issue with this candidate?*

- *Did this person get fired? If so, what's the reason, and is that the reason he had difficulty getting another job right away?*

Gaps in work history are a very common occurrence and can happen for a number of valid reasons. It can also happen for reasons that might not be as positive. When confronting this situation with your interviewer, be honest and explain the situation.

As I recommended in Chapter 7 (page 43), it is important that you provide in your credentials a written explanation of any gaps in work history. If you have done this, the issue will most likely not even come up, as the interviewer will have read your explanation and no longer considers your employment gaps an issue of concern. However, if it does remain an issue, refer to the explanation provided, reiterate that explanation during the interview, and address any further questions that the interviewer might have. Discuss everything you did to minimize the gap and steps you have taken to prevent a similar situation from happening in the future.

Let me stress that you should not hide a gap in your work history. Do not manipulate your credentials in any way to cover it up. Dishonesty and creative manipulation of your credentials will *always* come back to haunt you, and it's just not worth it.

Your Most Recent Position

An interviewer will almost always ask, "Why did your last employment opportunity end and what have you been doing since that time?" This question is raised for one of two reasons. You may have been in one of your recent positions (listed in your work history) for just a short period of time. In this situation, the interviewer wants to know if you were terminated from that position (and why), or if you left that job by your own choice (and why). The second reason the question gets raised is because the interviewer wants to know what about that past employer caused you to look for another job opportunity, to see if a similar situation is present.

When addressing this question, be honest (see a pattern here?). If your employment was terminated, take the time to explain the situation fully. The interviewer will check a reference at your past employer and *will* find out about the situation. Better for you to explain your perspective first.

If you left a past employer by personal choice, explain that situation as well. Use discretion in bad-mouthing a past employer in any way, as the interviewer will judge this negatively. (*Is that what the person would say about me if I have to fire them?*)

Other Topics

As you wrap up your discussion regarding your qualifications, you may want to address the following topics, which can be covered in a short period of time and will add to your overall positive impression.

Confirm why you are the best person (vs. other candidates) for the job.

When you are finished summarizing your qualifications, it is necessary to assess the interviewer's perception of you. You can come right out and ask directly: "Do you agree that my background and experience is appropriate for this position?"

You can also ask this way: "After confirming the responsibilities of the position and your expectations, I am comfortable that my experience and qualifications would allow me to be very successful in this position."

Or: "Is there any specific topic that you would like to discuss or clarify further?

When asking these questions, you are attempting to obtain the following from your interviewer:

- confirmation that you are a good fit for the position;

- additional questions or comments to address any outstanding concerns; and,

- affirmation of confidence in your qualifications and interest in the position.

Provide and review samples of your work, if applicable.

It's easy to talk about what you can do for your prospective employer before and during the interview process. Providing samples of your work shows how you bring actual value to this position and concretely supports how you can apply your past skills and experience in a practical manner. Make sure you have permission from past employers, customers or clients to share your work samples to demonstrate to the interviewer that you understand confidentiality agreements.

- First ask the interviewer if he would be interested in reviewing samples of your past work. Stress that you feel your work samples are *relevant* to the position being discussed, meaning they can be easily and immediately applied to the position responsibilities.

- Based upon your understanding of the expectations for the position, only show *relevant* work (again, applicable to the job responsibilities) that substantiates experience the interviewer is interested in. Sharing work samples that cannot be easily related to the position creates a negative perception in the mind of the interviewer.

- Have your work accessible, structured, and presented in a way to make it very easy for you and the interviewer to look at your work.

Summarizing Your Qualifications Makes a Difference

The time you spend with your interviewer discussing your qualifications can be productive in a short period of time. Your substantially prepared Summary of Qualifications will assist you, and more importantly the interviewer, in making the connection between your skills and experience and the company's expectations.

Throughout this stage of the interview, understand and confirm everything you need to know about the position, and confirm for the interviewer that you are the best candidate for the position. Address any issues or concerns about your credentials. The interviewer will be more comfortable than ever that the decision to bring you in for an interview was a good one.

Through your 60-Day Plan and *The First 60 Seconds*, you have made a substantial impression on the interviewer before you even sat down for the interview. What you have accomplished by presenting your qualifications will all but clinch the position for you (if not already).

CHAPTER 21

Continue Developing a Relationship with the Interviewer

What you will need:

Interview Agenda

I. Introductions

II. Discussion of Position
Requirements and Expectations

III. Review and Discussion of
Relevant Experience

➡ IV. Review and Discussion of
Non-Work Attributes

➡ V. Summary of Why You Are
Appropriate for the Position

VI. Follow Up and Next Steps

VII. Conclusion

*Personal
Profile*

*References
Summary*

Back in Chapter 17 (page 129), we discussed the importance of making a connection with the interviewer within the first 60 seconds of your meeting—to get the interviewer to think, "I really like this person." It was at that point that you initiated the process of developing a relationship with the interviewer. Throughout the interview process, you have the ability to substantiate and build upon that initial connection you made and further develop your relationship with your interviewer.

Relationships Are Everything

People work with other people who they like, and one person can like another for a thousand different reasons. If a person genuinely likes you, then there is the opportunity for them to develop trust, and if the person likes you and trusts you, they will most certainly want to work with you. Your objective as the interview proceeds is to further develop the relationship you initiated upon your first meeting and establish the basis for trust in you and in your abilities.

Information you collected and used to prepare your Personal Profile and your References Summary are the key tools in developing the relationship. Discuss and focus on both work and nonwork attributes you have, and provide a good feel for how you will adapt and function in the company work environment.

Using the Personal Profile in the Interview Setting

Any relationship you hope to develop with the interviewer has to be on a personal level. At the end of the day, interviewers are just like everyone else, regardless of their success and position in the company. They put their pants on one leg at a time, and you can be sure that there is something that you have in common. Your goal is to reach out to the interviewer, share something about yourself, and find that commonality. To develop a relationship effectively, *it has to be personal.*

The Personal Profile you prepared back in Section I included many nonwork attributes. Your Personal Profile was included in your credentials package, and it's very likely that your interviewer has reviewed it. Even so, the interview is a great opportunity to let the Personal Profile assist you in fostering a relationship with your interviewer.

Use your Personal Profile in the interview to share your nonwork passions and interests, and continue to develop your relationship.

You identified many personal attributes, including:

My Passions

First and foremost, let the interviewer know, and state it very clearly, that you have *passion*—about something, anything. Why? Because very few people share or discuss what they are truly passionate about. While you should certainly communicate passion for your work, you also need to express that you are passionate about something outside of the work environment. This is necessary for two reasons. First, in the interview setting, of course most people say they are passionate about their career. So that's not a differentiator. Talking about your nonwork passion *is a differentiator*, making it something you want to share with your interviewer. Second, nonwork interests give the interviewer a better sense of your personal qualities, and can also provide the opportunity for you to connect on a more personal level (maybe your interviewer has a similar or related passion).

My Hobbies and Special Interests

You may be wondering, *What's the difference between passions, hobbies, and special interests?* A "passion" is something you really care about and are totally committed to. It's not reasonable to be passionate about everything, so I look at hobbies and special interests as other activities you commit time to outside of work.

Sharing and discussing your hobbies and special interests can also help you make that personal connection. Plus, it provides an opportunity to learn something about the interviewer. While the person conducting the interview may or may not be passionate about anything, they must have some hobby or personal interest. Don't be afraid to inquire about them. If you accept the job offer for this position, you will have to work with this person, so you'd better like them.

Personal Development Activities

The personal development activities you listed may span both personal and professional development, and that's okay. The point you want to get across is your determined and conscious effort to develop yourself outside of the workplace. This speaks volumes about you as a person and is absolutely another differentiator.

My Family

Discussing family and friends is the easiest way to make a connection with another person, as we all have them. While you want to be cautious, so as not to cross the line of what might be considered too private or personal, sharing basic information about your family and friends is appropriate. You will find that the interviewer will likely take an interest and be willing to share some personal insight regarding family or friends.

References Are Available!

Providing professional references is the one thing that is not typically handled appropriately, in either the résumé development or the interview process. Professional references can be one of the most important criteria for selecting a candidate for an available position. For most hiring managers, it is an important consideration, but it is often taken into account far too late in the evaluation process. This is usually because the candidate included a statement on the résumé along the lines of "References–Available Upon Request."

Of course, you have already included your references, so direct the interviewer to your References Summary to substantiate your professional experience. Equally important, use the references to explain past colleague relationships you've developed.

When sharing with your prospective employer one or more of your references, highlight:

- the person's name, title, and company name;

- your relation to the person and the type of relationship you had with the person;

- how you developed a professional relationship, and also how you developed (an appropriate) personal relationship with the person; and,

- any characteristics of the person that you feel might be interesting or relative to your interviewer.

The References Summary you provide before and during the interview is another way for you *to differentiate yourself from your competition.* No one else will have gone to the effort of preparing them proactively or as thoroughly as you have. You have saved the interviewer from having to ask for them. Most importantly, using your References Summary will assist you in further developing a relationship with the interviewer.

Effectively use your References Summary during the interview.

Adapting Yourself to the Work Environment

One question that most hiring managers struggle with is whether the candidate will fit into the work environment. It is very difficult to answer that question by reviewing a résumé. It's difficult to make that assessment in an interview setting, even after multiple interviews. It usually isn't until after the candidate has been on the job for some period of time that the hiring manager can judge whether the person hired is in fact the appropriate person for the job. Unfortunately, by that time the hiring manager has already committed to the employee, so it is difficult to make a hiring change. As a result, hiring managers tend to be apprehensive about a hiring decision until they are somewhat comfortable that you can adapt effectively in the proposed work environment.

Early in my career as a hiring manager, I found it difficult to determine if a candidate would work out until after the person was on board. Unfortunately, like most managers, I did not have the luxury of waiting. I had to make a hiring decision based on my review of the person's credentials, references, and the results of the personal interview.

So is it possible to help the hiring manager obtain a better sense of how you will fit in if you are selected for the position? The answer is yes, and you must develop this understanding in the mind of your interviewer. You can accomplish this through a very simple three-step process:

1. Inquire as to the past challenges other people in this position may have had in adapting to their new responsibilities. If so, was it because of personal or professional reasons that the person did not work out as planned?

2. Share with the interviewer how you plan to overcome and address those challenges. You can include relevant experiences from your work history. Discuss your personal efforts to overcome similar situations in the past.

3. Ask the interviewer for her personal opinion on what it will take for the selected candidate to adapt to the position most effectively. Follow the reply you get with any skills or experiences you have that substantiate your ability to adapt as expected.

Anything you can do to help the hiring manager be comfortable about your ability to adapt to the work environment will make it easier for them to select you. It is a professional challenge for the hiring manager, but it is also a personal challenge. If the hiring manager selects you for the position, she will want you to be successful. Help the hiring manager be comfortable about your adaptability, and make it personal.

Develop a Relationship and Make It Personal

Relationships are everything. Following the suggestions in this chapter, along with some of your own, means that you will have made a great effort and had great success in further developing the relationship with your prospective employer. You also will have effectively addressed many of the challenges identified in Chapter 19 (page 145):

- *What are you really like?*

- *Will you fit into the environment?*

- *Do I like you?*

With the effective use of your Personal Profile and References Summary, along with your discussion of how you will adapt to the work environment, you will have addressed these questions and more.

You will have made it personal.

CHAPTER 22

Understand What's in It for You

What you will need:

Interview Agenda

I. Introductions
II. Discussion of Position
   Requirements and Expectations
III. Review and Discussion of
   Relevant Experience
IV. Review and Discussion of
   Non-Work Attributes
V. Summary of Why You Are
   Appropriate for the Position
VI. Follow-Up and Next Steps
VII. Conclusion

Company
Profile

Job
Profile

During the interview process, after you present your qualifications and establish a relationship with the person interviewing you, if there is time remaining you then have the opportunity to inquire more about what the benefits will be to you if you are offered and select the position.

This topic is saved for the end of the interview because, while important to you, what's in it for you is of least importance to the interviewer.

By the end of the interview, if your potential employer feels you have the necessary qualifications and they like you, you're in a great position. If there is time left, the interviewer will be happy to discuss your additional inquiries. If you have not satisfied the interviewer's expectations, then any discussion of what's in it for you may seem to be a waste of time, since the interviewer is not convinced of your viability as a candidate. Also, asking about how the job benefits you has the potential of overshadowing what's in it for them. In the end, it's the interviewer who makes the decision to select you, so satisfy him or her first.

What's more, if you effectively manage your 60-Day Plan, there is a high probability that the person interviewing you will already have a comprehensive understanding of your qualifications and your personal nonwork attributes. In that case, you will not need to devote as much time in the interview itself addressing those topics, and you can use the available remaining time to talk about topics you are interested in.

Using the Company and Job Profiles

Through the development of your Company and Job Profiles prior to the interview, you will already have a solid understanding of many of the position's job-related and employee-related benefits. In the interview, time permitting, you should inquire about any benefits for which you are unclear or need additional information about. Use the opportunity to ask about things that (a) *you really need to know* in order to make a sound decision, and (b) will convey to the interviewer that you have done your research, and already know about benefits that job candidates typically inquire about. Most importantly, do not make any inquiries that will change the interviewer's positive impression of you.

The Company and Job Profiles are designed to be working documents to assist in preparing your credentials. They have a secondary benefit in that they can be used to prepare your interview discussion questions. *Do not give these documents to the interviewer*, as they contain your personal comments and opinions about the company and the position. However, you may want to refer to them during the interview. In each of the profiles is a wealth of information about the company and the job that you can use to ask intelligent and insightful questions.

Reasonable Inquiries

To start discussing what's in it for you, simply ask, "Since we have addressed my experience and qualifications, would it be appropriate for us to discuss (insert your topic here)?". If the prerequisites are satisfied (which they will be), the interviewer will certainly oblige, and he or she will appreciate that you asked first.

Based on your research, you already know much of what you need to know. Use this time to ask reasonable questions that either clarify or probe.

For your interviewer, clarifying questions result in a clear understanding that you have researched the company, position, and benefits thoroughly. You will confirm that your understanding is accurate, or it will be improved by input from the interviewer. So the objective to the clarifying question is to *substantiate* your understanding to the interviewer and *gain clarity* through confirmation and further input from the interviewer.

Probing questions will solicit additional information. Your challenge here is to offer questions that are above and beyond what a typical candidate will ask. They need to be questions that give you an edge on how you are perceived as a candidate, as well as provide information about the company and position that most other candidates will not get. Asking these "appropriate" questions is just one more way to continue *to differentiate yourself from your competition.*

Let's take a moment to review some types of additional information that is reasonable to ask about.

 Ask appropriate clarifying and probing questions to solicit and understand what's in it for you.

Growth in Responsibilities over Time

You want to let it be known that because you understand the responsibilities of the position fully, you have confidence in your abilities to satisfy the job requirements. When you do, you are going to ask for more responsibility. Managers find it difficult to say "no" to someone who takes the initiative to ask for more. Let the person know that you would expect to get to that point, and inquire as to what growth opportunities or responsibilities might be. Let your potential employer know that you are not the worker who meets only what's required, and ensure that the manager will not limit your opportunities to a narrow scope of responsibilities.

Growth in Responsibilities within the Position

You might ask, "I'm sure there have been many successful people in this position who have gone on to do other great things for you (the manager) within the department. Can you share with me one of those examples or what an aggressive career path might look like?" If you are interviewing with the hiring manager you will ultimately be working for, limit your questions to growth and opportunity within the department *under* his or her span of control. Unfortunately, there are people who become nervous or threatened when someone talks about challenging their position or moving beyond them.

Employee Benefits

As a general rule, the discussion of employee benefits should be left for a later time. Typically the hiring manager or interviewer does not have enough information to answer your questions completely, and it's reasonable to assume that they might not be very interested in the topic.

However, what you can do is convey that you have already researched and understand the employee benefits package, which they will be interested in knowing and appreciate that they do not have to address that topic with you. It is also helpful to ask the interviewer what they like most about the benefits. You could ask, "Is there one employee benefit that you like, are most impressed with, or feel is unique to this company?" In this case, you are asking for their personal opinion and their response might provide a unique perspective about employee benefits.

Your Link to Department and Corporate Goals

Your hope is to interview with a person who has a commitment to the goals of the department and the company. If that is the case, you want it to be understood that you have a similar appreciation and commitment, and given that, you want to know how your role will help the department meet its goals. In essence you want to ask how your daily responsibilities will help make your manager and the department (and subsequently the company) more successful. Managers love people who make them more successful.

How Your Accomplishments Will Be Evaluated

This inquiry is important because you want the person to know that you are a results-driven and goal-oriented worker. As such, you want to ask if there is the potential to work together to define specific goals that you personally manage and work toward throughout the evaluation period. You want to gain a sense of whether there is an objective evaluation process and set of evaluation criteria in place.

Other Questions to Consider

- "Can you share with me your perspective regarding the growth prospects for the company?"

- "Are there other ways for you, me, and the department to make a difference for the company?"

- "Are there other ways that I would be able to make you and the department more successful?"

Inquiries to Leave for Later

There are a variety of topics that in most cases should not be addressed during the interview and are best suited for discussion after you receive the job offer. It is not that these topics are unimportant—they are, and you want them addressed before you decide to accept the position. Asking these questions during the interview will not increase your chances of being selected for the position. If asking a specific question provides no job selection benefits or does not improve how the interviewer perceives you, then do not ask that question during the interview. Do not ask a question just for the sake of asking it— make sure you ask only good questions.

Non-beneficial questions are those your competition will most likely ask during the interview, such as: "Do you have health insurance?" or "How much vacation and sick time do employees get?"

Let the other candidates go ahead and use their valuable interview time asking these types of questions. You will be using your questions to your advantage.

Again, if you feel that a particular question will not actually improve your chances of being selected for the position, address the question after you have received an offer for the position. At that time, you can follow up with the hiring manager, the HR department, or other people within the company. Let's discuss some of these follow-up topics and why they are better suited for a later time.

Promotion Opportunities within the Department

While this is a genuinely appropriate topic to discuss, it can sometimes be viewed negatively. A hiring manager may be uncomfortable talking about your next position within the company when you have not yet been considered for the position at hand. You have already addressed this indirectly by inquiring about *career growth* and *growth in responsibilities* and even with the topic of *how you will be evaluated*. The interviewer may have already offered additional information about promotion opportunities.

Promotion Opportunities and Career Growth within the Company

The hiring manager is interested in determining your viability for a position within her department—right now—and is hoping that if you are selected, you will be a valuable asset for her for a reasonable amount of time. Discussions that delve into opportunities beyond the department can indicate that you may not be committed to the position available and may be looking for something other than what is currently available. That may be the case, but there's no need to worry the hiring manager who is trying to make a decision to hire you.

Compensation

Compensation is arguably one of the most important considerations for any job candidate. But compensation only becomes a topic of discussion if and when the position is offered to you. You should have already researched the position's compensation range. Save your questions, comments, and negotiating position until after they have committed to you—until they want you.

Vacation and Sick Time

Sometimes discussions about vacation and sick time can make the interviewer wonder, *Why is this person so interested in time off? Do they typically take a lot of sick time? Is the amount of vacation time our company provides going to be an issue for this person and impact his or her desire to accept the position if offered?* You can address remaining questions about vacation and sick time with HR or the hiring manager once you have received the job offer.

Work Schedule and Travel

This topic can go either way. You want the hiring manager to know you are comfortable with and committed to the work schedule and travel expectations of the position so that they select you. At the same time, you do not want to raise any concerns you may have, like working overtime or excessive travel. "Concerns" make hiring managers nervous. They may be able to address your concerns better after they have committed to you.

Any Perceived Negative Aspects of the Position

On your Job Profile, you may have identified one or more negative aspects of the position that might be of concern to you or that make you uncomfortable. It is not necessary to make your concerns the interviewer's concerns until after you are selected for the position.

Addressing Challenges That May Arise

It is possible that regardless of your approach and how conscientious you are about the topics and questions you raise, there may be concerns and questions in the mind of the interviewer. You will be able to read the interviewer's reaction to the questions you ask and will know if you need to address the topic further before the interview ends.

The biggest challenge that may arise is that your questions could, at least temporarily, overshadow some of the positive aspects of the preceding interview. That is not how you want to leave the interview. Just to be thorough, as you close this aspect of the interview, offer to the interviewer the following:

1. "Considering all that we discussed today, is there anything that is of concern to you that would prevent you from considering me for this position?"

2. "Thank you for answering all of my questions. I am more comfortable than ever that this would be a great opportunity for me."

Raising these questions gives you a final opportunity to address any last concerns of the interviewer and leave him or her with your full confidence in your desire for the position.

CHAPTER 23

I'm Available!
What's Next?

Eventually, the interview must end. Hopefully, as it comes to a close, you will feel that it has been a fantastic experience, and you will be confident that all of your hard work and preparation has proven beneficial. There are just two more items to address before you head home to wait for your job offer: tell them your availability and confirm the next steps of the process.

I'm Available!

Telling the interviewer that you are available seems obvious and maybe even redundant, but I can assure you that many times the manager is left with an unclear impression at the end of an interview. Why would that be? If you are there interviewing for the position, you must be available and interested, right?

Oddly enough, that is not always the case. The interviewer might get the impression that you are not really interested. Hiring managers have seen enough situations to substantiate this type of feeling. From the hiring manager's perspective, it's possible that a candidate is just exploring options. Maybe the candidate is really more interested in another position at another company. Maybe the candidate already has a firm offer from a competing company. Maybe as the interview progressed, the candidate had a change of heart. There could be many reasons why the interviewer could feel that you might not be interested, and that is not how you want to end the interview. Hiring managers have all experienced the situation when they have made an offer to a candidate, only for it to be declined. If the hiring manager has the impression that you are not 110 percent interested in the position—even if they really want you—they may not go to the trouble of preparing an offer for fear that it will be a waste of time.

You must let them know that you are very interested in the position.

As the interview comes to a close, it is not unusual for the interviewer to come right out and ask the question, "Are you interested and available?" At that point, what are some of the things that could give the impression that you might not be available or interested in the position?

Any Answer Other Than "YES!"

It's simple. The interviewer wants to hear "yes," and you need to be sure to say it, and say it very clearly, "YES, I am interested and available!"

A Long Transition or Start Time

The interviewer wants to know that if he or she goes to the trouble of offering you the position, not only will you accept it, but you will start work within a reasonable amount of time. As the interview comes to a close, when they have all but officially selected you for the position, you do not want to share anything except, "I'm available with two weeks notice to my company." That response is expected and reasonable. Telling the interviewer that you want to wait until you get your bonus six weeks from now is not expected and not reasonable. If you have circumstances that prevent you from starting a new job right away, share those circumstances with your prospective employer later, after you have received the job offer and figured out a way to remove those roadblocks or address those circumstances more effectively.

Other Opportunities You Are Considering

Most hiring managers understand that a candidate is most likely simultaneously considering other opportunities. That does not mean that the hiring manager is comfortable with that possibility. Let the hiring manager know that there is no opportunity for you more important than this one. If you are interviewing with other companies or even have another job offer, save that information for a later time—until you receive an offer from the company you are interviewing with now or until you need to make a follow-up communication.

Planned Upcoming Vacations

It is not unusual or unreasonable that you might have a vacation planned sometime in the near future. Most every company has a waiting period before you are permitted to take time off, and the hiring manager does not want to hear that you need two weeks of vacation after a short time in your new position. Many times a hiring manager will postpone an offer until you are available, after your vacation, or may remove you from consideration to avoid dealing with your situation. If a planned vacation is an issue for you, discuss it only after you have a job offer and work closely with your prospective manager to address the situation together.

The situations above can all be considered roadblocks to your potential hiring. Refrain from raising any issues or concerns when doing so is really unnecessary. You may have a valid concern or issue, but it is really only a concern or issue if you are offered the position. Get the job offer first, and then work closely with your prospective manager and company personnel to address your concerns in an appropriate manner.

To bring the interview to a close, share with your interviewer the following:

- "I am very interested in the position (with one or two specific reasons why)."

- "I am available to start work immediately."

It is important that the interviewer understand clearly that this position is the only position you are interested in and that there is absolutely no reason why you would not accept a job offer if one was presented to you.

Leave the interviewer with the clear understanding that you are interested in the position available, and that there is nothing that would prevent you from accepting the position if offered.

What's Next?

The final step in your interview process is to ask two brief questions: to review and confirm any follow-up activities and discuss the next steps in the process. At the end of the interview, given that in most cases your interviewer's valuable time has dissipated, the candidate tends to forget these two questions. The questions can be addressed quickly, and you really need this information before you leave the interview.

Question 1: Follow-Up Items

Ask the interviewer, "Are there any items that you would like me to follow up with you on?" This can be for both you and the interviewer, but you certainly want to discuss and confirm items that you need to address. Some of the more common follow-up activities include:

- additional information regarding past recent and relevant experience;

- additional prior work samples that can help show your ability to effectively complete the work of the new position;

- additional professional reference information; and,

- information to address any questions you could not completely answer during the interview. **Note:** This is very important! During the interview be sure to note these questions. We will address them further in the next section.

Question 2: Next Steps

Ask the interviewer, "What are the next steps in your hiring process?" This is also a reasonable question, and the interviewer will be comfortable explaining how the process will work. What you specifically want to know is:

- "When will any remaining interviews be completed?"

- "How many other candidates are being considered for the position?"

- "Do you plan to have a second round of interviews before making your decision?"

- "When do you need to make a decision and when would you like the person to start work?"

- "When can I expect to hear from you?"

It may appear that these are a lot of questions for you to ask right at the end of the interview, and depending on how the interview transpired that may be true. You may find that there is only time for one question, or you may find yourself asking them as you are walking out of the interviewer's office. If you have time, ask as much as you can. If you are unable to have all your questions addressed, don't worry; while not an optimal option, you still have another opportunity to address your questions as part of your follow-up communications that we will address in the next chapter.

That brings us to the end of the interview process. Your executed 60-Day Plan is behind you, and you have managed your first 60 seconds and your prospective employer's interview process. After following the strategies outlined in this and previous chapters, your prospective employer can be thinking only one thing:

Wow, that candidate is really different from all the rest, and I have got to get that person on my team!

Congratulations. Now you just have to wait for the job offer. Don't worry—the offer will come quickly.

Section 4

The Close

Finis coronat opus. [The end crowns the work]
—*Anonymous*

Of a good beginning cometh a good end.
—*John Heywood*

CHAPTER 24

Post-Interview Communications

It's the end of the day, and you're in your living room, relaxing and recalling the great day you've just had. Your interview is behind you, and you cannot help but smile as you think about your successes and accomplishments. All of your efforts have paid off as you think about how effective your *First 60 Seconds* presentation was and how you were able to substantiate and differentiate yourself as the primary candidate for the job. Now all that's left is to wait patiently for the formal job offer to arrive.

What should you do until then? Get up off the couch and get back to your desk or computer. There is important business to attend to.

Your post-interview communications with your prospective employer cannot be overlooked. These communications, which you will compose now, and the others over the next several days and weeks, will continue to solidify your professionalism and attention to detail. The communications allow you to continue and extend the relationship you established with the hiring manager and other interview participants. Most importantly, the post-interview communications continue to differentiate you as the candidate of choice.

You may be asking yourself, "Can a post-interview communication really be a differentiator?" The answer is most certainly, "YES!"

The post-interview communication can be a differentiator for several reasons. First, not every job candidate who has completed an interview will send a follow-up communication *of any kind* to the hiring manager. In reality, a large percentage of job candidates will not send any type of communication, either because they are not interested in the job, feel they are not being seriously considered, are lazy, or just did not think about it.

Second, even if everyone you are competing with were to send a follow-up communication, you can still differentiate yourself by your timing, content, thoroughness, presentation, and approach.

Finally, plan an ongoing communication process with your prospective employer to effectively bridge the gap from the time your interview ends until the first day of your new job. If you follow the suggestions in this chapter, you can rest assured that no one else will be as diligent and as comprehensive in their post-interview activities as you.

The post-interview communication process includes much more than a single letter or communication after the interview. The time from completing your interview until receiving a job offer can span anywhere from a day to several weeks. Because you have effectively followed *The First 60 Seconds* approach, the time frame should be relatively short, because your prospective employer really wants you and will not want you to get away. However, if you felt that your interview did not go particularly well, or it seems to be taking a little longer to get a response from your prospective employer, do not despair. A number of circumstances may cause a delay in an employer's ability to send you a job offer. The hiring manager may need to complete remaining interviews, confer with other interview participants, or work through the formal HR department process.

While you wait for the job offer to arrive, there are many unique methods you can use to keep the lines of communication open, including:

- Post-Interview Letter

- Thank-You Letter or Note Card

- Secondary Follow-Up Letter

- Notice of Offer (from another company)

- Acceptance of Offer (from another company)

Exhibit 24.1
Post-Interview Communication Process

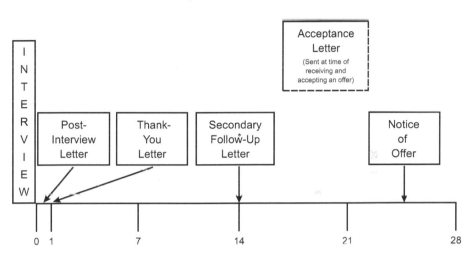

DAYS

The different communications are developed at various times over a potential month-long time frame as suggested above.

The objectives of your post-interview communication approach will be to:

- Convey professionalism, thoroughness, and attention to detail.

- Maintain ongoing relationship development.

- Promote ongoing differentiation.

The Post-Interview Letter

You will prepare the Post-Interview Letter within twenty-four hours of your first interview. Why the hurry? It is important to prepare it while the interview is still fresh in your mind. Moreover, you want to expediently reestablish communication with the hiring manager to solidify why you are the most appropriate candidate for the position. You need to realize that while the interview may have been your sole focus for the last several days or weeks, the hiring manager was most likely interviewing other candidates, managing staff, completing regular work responsibilities, and dealing with dozens of other work and personal issues. Therefore, it is important that you take the time to assist the hiring manager, while still fresh in his or her mind, in remembering clearly your positive aspects, including skills and experience, and why you are the candidate of choice.

Through the Post-Interview Letter you also have the opportunity to clarify or make additional points that you may not have been able to convey during the interview, either because you ran out of time or you did not think about it. Consider the Post-Interview Letter as an extension of the interview. It's an opportunity to make a final summation and provide your closing remarks for the hiring manager—again.

Preparing and providing the Post-Interview Letter to the hiring manager will satisfy the following objectives:

- Thank the interviewer for taking time out of a busy day to meet with you.

- Confirm you understand the position.

- Express that you are a qualified candidate by summarizing and providing specific justification.

- Recap main interview points.

- Summarize follow-up activities.

- Express that you are interested, excited, and available.

Refer to Exhibit 24.2 for a sample format of the Post-Interview Letter.

While you want to send out the letter soon after your interview, you do not want to prepare something in haste that will be considered unprofessional or sloppy—you have done too much to detract from

Exhibit 24.2
The Post-Interview Letter

Month DD, YYYY

Mr. John Smith
XYZ Corporation
1234 North Shore Drive
My Town, IL 12345-6789

Dear Mr. Smith:

I would like thank you for taking the time to meet with me (today/yesterday/date). The interview was an interesting and exciting process, and I learned a great deal about you and your organization.

I feel our discussion solidified my understanding of the position, and I feel I am a very qualified candidate for the following reasons:

- Reason 1
- Reason 2
- Reason 3

Based on our discussion there are several things that we agreed required follow-up on my part. I have addressed the items noted and will follow up shortly with the remaining information.

- Item 1 (additional information attached/forthcoming)
- Item 2 (additional information attached/forthcoming)
- Item 3 (additional information attached/forthcoming)

Mr. Smith, I am genuinely interested in the opportunity we discussed and I am available to start work immediately should you conclude that I am the most appropriate candidate. I am excited at the prospect of working with you and your team.

Thank you very much for your consideration, and I look forward to hearing from you.

Sincerely,

Your Name
(123) 456-7890
yourname@email.com

the positive impression you have created. Take your time and prepare a letter that conveys professionalism and differentiation from the other candidates.

When people do prepare a follow-up communication, it is typically an email, and it is quickly sent off. That can be a big mistake. Unfortunately, email as a form of communication tends to lose quite a bit of the formality, grammar, and punctuation detail found in a formal, professional business letter. You are going to prepare a full professional letter, using the format provided or one of your own. Of course, you should save it in a standard electronic format.

If you email the letter to the hiring manager, do not skip the process of creating a formal business letter. The best option is to send your letter as an attachment. However, if you decide to paste it in the body of an email, ensure that the letter's formatting remains intact.

When sending the letter via email, also send the letter in hard-copy form. As explanation for sending two letters, refer to the copy that was sent via email. Suggest you know how full everyone's inbox is these days, making it easy to miss emails, so you wanted to send a hard copy as well. It is preferable to send the hard copy using a delivery service that tracks the delivery to a specific person.

Sending your letter via email and in hard copy provides several benefits. It allows you the opportunity to have two different communication-connection points with the hiring manager at two different times, it provides a hard copy of the letter to the hiring manager for inclusion in your file, and the hard-copy is insurance against the possibility that the email you sent is lost or not read.

Finally, the letter should be sent to the primary decision maker, which is typically the hiring manager. While there may be other participants from HR and the rest of the organization, it is the hiring manager that you must maintain your communication with.

Prepare a Post-Interview Letter within twenty-four hours of your first interview.

Thank-You Letter or Note Card

The Thank-You Letter or Note Card is an additional way for you to communicate with the hiring manager. It does not replace the

Post-Interview Letter, but more appropriately is written as a follow-up to it. I especially like the Thank You Letter or Note Card as a way to send a personal, handwritten note to the other interview participants. It is a great way to reach out to those people who, while not the primary decision makers, may have the ability to provide input to the hiring manager regarding your viability as a candidate.

Writing a Thank-You Letter or Note Card will satisfy the following objectives:

- Thank the interviewer for taking time out of his or her busy day to meet with you.

- Tell the interviewer that you enjoyed meeting him or her and that you look forward to working with them.

- Allow you to include other interviewers, while not the primary decision maker, in the overall process.

- Allow you to provide the interviewer something to remember you by.

It is extremely important that the letter or note be *handwritten* and *mailed*. While this approach may seem a bit archaic, that's kind of the point. When was the last time you received a handwritten letter or note? It is unquestionably a dying art, and the handwritten note will certainly be differentiator for you. Also, it provides the opportunity for the person receiving the note to get it in a non-email form that they can open, hold, and keep. We all know that emails get lost, overlooked, and sometimes completely disregarded. Also, all email correspondence looks the same.

The thank-you note should go to everyone who participated in the interview process: representatives from HR, team members, customers, etc. You will be surprised to find how well received it will be and how quickly it will get back to the hiring manager that you sent them out. The note should be brief, personalized, and professional. Here is an example of a personal message you might write:

Dear Ms. Robinson,

It was a pleasure to meet you at my interview on _____.
Thank you for your time and consideration. I hope to have the opportunity
to work with you very soon.

Sincerely,

Your Name

It requires a little extra effort, but take the time to send out personalized thank-you notes to each of the interview participants. People always appreciate a thank-you, and odds are no one else (your competition) will even think to do it. Even if they all do, your personalized note will still be unique—written in your hand and in your own words. The personalized note requires a small investment and it can produce great returns. *It is a great differentiator.*

 Send a handwritten Thank-You Letter or Note Card to all interview participants.

The Secondary Follow-Up Letter

After two weeks have passed, or after the time the hiring manager expected to make a decision has lapsed, it may be necessary to send a follow-up communication to again establish contact with the hiring manager.

The Secondary Follow-Up Letter should be used sparingly and cautiously. It will be your second and only additional follow-up communication with the hiring manager, unless further communications are requested from the manager or company. The last thing a hiring manager wants is to be continually pestered while trying to complete the interviewing and selection process. At the same time, a single follow-up letter after a couple of weeks is reasonable.

While you may not think so, a prospective employer may have a very good reason for not contacting you. The purpose of the Secondary Follow-Up Letter is to establish contact in order to determine the status of the selection and hiring process. Like the Post-Interview Letter, this communication can be sent via email.

Objectives of the Secondary Follow-Up Letter:

• Reestablish contact with the hiring manager.

- Inquire as to the status of the interviewing and selection process.

- Inquire as to the need for additional information.

- Let the potential employer know that you are interested and available.

- Thank the person for their time and consideration.

Refer to Exhibit 24.3 on page 196 for a sample of the Secondary Follow-Up Letter.

The response can give you a better idea of the status of the selection process. If the hiring manager responds to you directly, the status will be very clear, and this will most often be the case. Sometimes, however, the hiring manager for some reason may decide not to respond. No response can also provide a sense of the status. It is possible that the hiring manager never received your inquiry, is extremely busy, or just does not want to talk to you and that can be because you are not being considered. Or it may mean that you are being considered and there is just nothing to report at the time. Regardless, the Secondary Follow-Up Letter is necessary if you have not received an offer or a status within two weeks from the time of your interview.

Notice of Offer

The Notice of Offer is another communication that you may find necessary to prepare, and it can be used for a number of situations.

Notice of Offer from Another Company

If you have received an offer, it is best to let other companies know as soon as possible. The primary reason is that if you have interviewed with multiple companies, there is likely another company that may be interested in you—they may just not have had the opportunity to get in touch with you regarding an offer of employment. As you will note in the example, the intent is to sincerely let the other company know that not only have you received another offer, but that you are still very interested in the position they have and would like to be considered. You may find that you will receive one or more counteroffers.

Refer to Exhibit 24.4 on page 197 for a sample of the Notice of Offer from Another Company.

Exhibit 24.3
Secondary Follow-Up Letter

Month DD, YYYY

Mr. John Smith
XYZ Corporation
1234 North Shore Drive
My Town, IL 12345-6789

Dear Mr. Smith:

It has been two weeks since the time we last spoke. I can imagine that your schedule is quite hectic trying to complete the interviewing and selection process for your open position while managing your regular duties. If it is not too much of an imposition, I would like to inquire as to the status of your selection process.

If there is any additional information that I could provide to more fully clarify why I feel I am the best person for the job, please do not hesitate to ask. Additionally, if you feel it would be helpful to have a follow-up discussion regarding the position and my qualifications, I would be happy to meet with you as your schedule permits.

Mr. Smith, I would like to reiterate that I am very interested in the position we discussed and would welcome the opportunity to work with you and your team.

Thank you very much for your consideration, and I look forward to hearing from you soon.

Sincerely,

Your Name
(123) 456-7890
yourname@email.com

Exhibit 24.4
Notice of Offer from Another Company

Month DD, YYYY

Mr. John Smith
XYZ Corporation
1234 North Shore Drive
My Town, IL 12345-6789

Dear Mr. Smith:

I wanted to let you know that I have received an offer letter for an employment opportunity with another company.

As I hopefully have conveyed to you during my interview and other communications, I am very interested in working with you and your organization, and that is still the case. I feel that my skills and qualifications would allow me to be a valuable asset to the organization and I am confident that I would be both productive and successful from the start.

If you feel you still have interest in considering me as a candidate, please let me know at your earliest convenience. I would appreciate the opportunity to talk with you further.

Thank you again for taking the time to meet with me on <u>Month, DD</u>. I really enjoyed talking with you about your organization and learning more about the opportunities within your department.

I look forward to hearing from you.

Sincerely,

Your Name
(123) 456-7890
yourname@email.com

Acceptance of Offer from Another Company

If you have received an offer from another company you are planning to accept, it is necessary to let other companies you have interviewed with know your intentions. I always suggest that this communication go out to the other companies at least twenty-four hours before you actually accept the offer, as you may find that other companies respond immediately with an offer to consider.

Refer to Exhibit 24.5 for a sample of the Acceptance of Offer from Another Company.

No Longer Interested in the Position

Sometimes it is also necessary to let a company know that you are simply no longer interested in a position you interviewed for. You may have decided to postpone or end your job search or the position may no longer meet your original expectations. Regardless of the reason, it is professional courtesy to let the company know your decision. Even though you are no longer interested in the particular position or the company right now, you may want to pursue other opportunities at a later date, and it is best to maintain a professional and positive impression and relationship. For this situation you can use the No Longer Interested in the Position sample provided in Exhibit 24.6 on page 200.

 Use the recommended communication options to professionally conclude your job search process with a company you have interviewed with.

Exhibit 24.5
Acceptance of Offer from Another Company

Month DD, YYYY

Mr. John Smith
XYZ Corporation
1234 North Shore Drive
My Town, IL 12345-6789

Dear Mr. Smith:

I would like to take a brief moment to let you know that I have concluded my job search and have accepted a position with another company. It was an exciting process and I am looking forward to my new career opportunity.

I appreciate you taking the time to meet with me back on Month, DD. I really enjoyed talking with you about your organization and learning more about the opportunities within your department.

I hope that the success of your organization continues in the years to come.

Sincerely,

Your Name
(123) 456-7890
yourname@email.com

Exhibit 24.6
No Longer Interested in the Position

Month DD, YYYY

Mr. John Smith
XYZ Corporation
1234 North Shore Drive
My Town, IL 12345-6789

Dear Mr. Smith:

I would like to take a brief moment to let you know that I have concluded my job search.

I appreciate you taking the time to meet with me back on <u>Month, DD.</u> I really enjoyed talking with you about your organization and learning more about the opportunities within your department.

I hope that the success of your organization continues in the years to come.

Sincerely,

Your Name
(123) 456-7890
yourname@email.com

CHAPTER 25

The Offer Letter and Employment Agreement

Verbal Offer = Offer Letter = Contract =
Employment Agreement = *Your Future*

The day has finally arrived. After all of your hard work, the job offer is now before you. All that is left is to review and fully understand the offer as presented and decide whether you wish to accept it. That sounds simple enough, but there is very important work to be done to appropriately finish your job search effort.

The job offer can come in many forms. It may be verbal, a letter, or an employment agreement/contract—or a combination of forms at different times. Maybe you will receive an offer letter first, followed by a complete and detailed agreement. Every company's form can be different, but what's important is the offer's content. There are certain conditions, details, and agreements you want to be sure are understood clearly and confirmed.

Everything you have done up until this point was in an effort to get the job offer. Once you have it, it is very easy to get excited about your new offer and the prospects for big bucks and even bigger career opportunities. As a result, you might go ahead and accept an offer quickly once it has been presented, forgoing the details of the actual employment arrangement so that you will not miss out on this great opportunity.

Resist the urge to react and decide quickly!

It is perfectly normal to be excited; you have earned it and you are in an excellent position. But the most important thing for you to do is *take the time to carefully review your new employment agreement.* You have been diligent in your efforts to execute *The First 60 Seconds* approach so far, and you are going to show that same diligence regarding your employment offers.

Your ultimate objective is to get everything you want while providing your new employer with everything they want. It is possible, and the best scenario, for you to begin your new career with your new employer with a sound, fair, and reasonable employment agreement.

> Take the time to review and fully understand the employment agreement or job offer as presented. It is your future, and you have earned the right to take the time you need to review it appropriately.

Take time to review your job offer in a straightforward, logical, and reasonable manner. Remember, you have the offer, you are in the driver's seat, and you are in an enviable position (your competition is still waiting). You have the ability to solidify the details of your employment to be beneficial to both you and your employer. It's easy to get overexcited, to overanalyze, and to subsequently lose focus on what is really important to you. Your timing, negotiation, discussion, and the final agreement simply need to be reasonable and logical—for you and your employer. Take that approach and the process will go smoothly.

The Employer's Perspective

Let's take a moment to think about what might be going through the mind of your employer. Because you have been extended an offer, the company obviously wants you. Your prospective employer has just completed a fairly extensive process that included justification and approval of the position, advertising, collecting and reviewing résumés, scheduling and conducting numerous interviews with several candidates, extensive interaction with HR, and much deliberation. The process spanned at least several weeks and the hiring manager is relieved to have an appropriate candidate—*you*—for the position. In the hiring manager's mind, the process is complete; all that is needed is your approval. You have proven to be the best candidate for the position. You can be assured that the hiring manager does not want to continue the interviewing process and wants nothing more than to have you fill the position.

If that sounds like you might be in a pretty good negotiating position, you probably are. A few major factors affect how a hiring manager approaches employment negotiations.

Need to Finalize Everything Right Away

The hiring manager wants the position closed quickly so that he or she can move on with other responsibilities. The company wants you and will continue to want you as long as you cooperate to finalize the employment arrangement within a reasonable amount of time and without being tremendously difficult. Otherwise, while not the intention, the hiring manager may need to move on to the next potential candidate. You have some time, and you are in a great position—just be reasonable.

Take It or Leave It Mentality

Most companies have a standard employment agreement, and in the interest of time (and avoiding additional effort), the hiring manager will want to minimize the number of changes to it. That's understandable. However, companies do expect that there will be some changes made to the agreement, if minimally, for the variables of the person and the position. They also realize that some of the content may require discussion or further clarification. You will not be the first person to request a modification to the company's employment agreement. In fact, there likely have been hundreds before you that have done it, and have successfully made changes to the standard agreement.

Need to Keep a Level Playing Field

Every manager attempts to keep employment arrangements equitable ("everyone in this position is paid the same") among all the individuals within specific positions or job-grade levels. This is partially driven by employment standards enforced by the company and HR, and by the fact that the manager does not want to deal with personnel issues that may result from any inequity. However, managers make exceptions all the time, especially with excellent candidates. The manager's desire for internal compensation equity should not deter you from asking for what you want.

Difficulty of Filling the Position

You may have obtained a sense of this during your interview. Simply put, the more critical the position, the more difficult the hiring process, the more interested and flexible the hiring manager will be in working with you to finalize the employment arrangements.

Interest in Your Long-Term Potential

Once the position is filled, the hiring manager does not want to worry about that position again for quite some time. The manager has considered your potential not only in meeting the immediate needs of the position within the department, but also what you may be able to contribute over the long-term—a two- to five-year period. The hiring manager may be thinking not only about your current employment arrangement, but also what he or she may need to do to keep you with the company. The considered time frame can have a direct impact on the structure of the original employment agreement—to the benefit of both parties.

A Number of Other Qualified Candidates

You can assume that there was at least one other candidate considered for the position, and the hiring manager may even suggest that there were a number of qualified candidates. That may be true, but if you have received the offer, you are *the only* candidate being considered. Companies typically do not extend offers to multiple candidates for the same position, so as long as your offer is on the table, you are the one candidate they want.

"My Hands Are Tied"

You will undoubtedly hear this at least once during your career lifetime. It is a simple technique where the hiring manager claims to defer the authority and responsibility for the hiring decision to someone else—fictional or real. The idea is that if the hiring manager cannot help you, then whatever issue or question you raised just goes away. In some cases, the hiring manager may indeed be controlled or influenced by someone else, including a boss or the HR department. You just may need to reiterate or solidify why you were selected and why you are the best person for the job. Remember, this is a hiring *manager*, which means this person most likely has the authority to make the final decision about your employment arrangement—in other words, the manager's hands are never completely bound.

The Employee's (YOUR) Perspective

Both you and your prospective employer have the same end goal, although you may be considering different factors to reach that goal. The company wants you, and you want to work for the company. All of your effort and the job offer in front of you solidify that fact. Everything else, some of which may be important and some not so important, will not change that fact.

While the hiring manager has much to consider in an effort to finalize the employment arrangement with you, there are certainly a number of things that could be going through your mind as you consider your next career move. Let's look at some of the things you might consider as you evaluate a job offer:

I need to act now or I might lose the opportunity.

This is a very common reaction for anyone who receives a job offer. Unless you decline the offer or extend the time frame for accepting the offer to an unreasonable length (longer than one week), you will not lose the opportunity. Take it easy, take your time, rationally and thoroughly review your offer, and keep your prospective employer informed of your progress to reaching an answer.

I want to get to work and get started.

Maybe you have been out of work for a while, you are frustrated with your current job, or maybe you are just excited about the idea of pursuing a new career opportunity. Like the hiring manager, you have invested a significant amount of time and effort and are looking forward to finishing the job search process. That's understandable, but do not let that fact influence your approach to evaluating your job offer. You have waited this long, and you have some time to make a sound decision.

I want satisfying work and a satisfying work environment.

You want your next career opportunity to be both satisfying and support your long-term career objectives. You want the work environment to be challenging, friendly, and supportive, as you will spend a significant portion of each working day in that environment. In the excitement of receiving and reviewing your job offer, keep these objectives under consideration.

I want appropriate compensation and standard benefits.

You want to receive fair and reasonable compensation for your work. Based on your research, prior experiences, skills, and knowledge of the position offered, you should have a good idea of the compensation to expect and ultimately what you can obtain. There is also a standard of employee benefits you need to support your living requirements. You're good, but keep your expectations reasonable, and understand you should be able to get what you want—within reason.

Appropriate compensation and benefits keep pace with inflation and the cost of living, and they are guided by an employer's job or grade levels and salary ranges. They should also be in line with local market and industry salary ranges and benefits guidelines.

Now I can stop all of my other job search efforts.

A typical and immediate reaction upon receiving a job offer is to stop other job search efforts. Your current job offer is not finalized, and your new career opportunity does not begin until you actually start your new job—your first day of work. You would hate to decline another job offer only to find out the week before you start your new job that the company has had to initiate cutbacks and your position has been eliminated. Continue your job search efforts until your new career opportunity is finalized.

I need to be willing to walk away.

This is arguably the most difficult thing to think about. After all of your efforts, you have been successful and received the job offer you desired. However, you need to be fully comfortable with the opportunity and the details of your employment arrangement. You may already have another offer to consider or another may be coming. You need to work closely and cooperatively with your prospective employer to finalize the details of your employment, but do not force yourself into a job where you will not be happy or comfortable.

Employment Agreement Considerations

An employment agreement can be overwhelming. Even the simplest agreement contains details that are extremely important to your future, including compensation, benefits, and job responsibilities. Conversely, the standard employment agreement of a large corporation can exceed ten pages and is loaded with legal terminology that may appear to be broad and include vague clauses. Do not despair. Again, you are most likely not the first person to be offered this agreement, and in most cases, the details effectively define the employment arrangement and protect the interests of both you and your employer.

That does not mean you should go ahead and just sign the agreement without reading it. More appropriately, take the time to review each word of the agreement to your complete understanding. We're going to spend some time reviewing many of the most popular components of a standard employment agreement and how you might approach negotiating those components.

Exhibit 25.1 on page 208 provides a list of the many considerations for you to keep in mind as you review and evaluate your employment agreement. It is a fairly extensive list. While not meant to be all encompassing, it will provide you with a sound understanding of what you may be confronted with.

The details provided in your specific employment agreement or situation can certainly benefit the employer, the employee, or both. Focus on items that provide a win-win for you and your employer. At the same time, it is appropriate and necessary for you to look out for your own best interests.

There are key items that you need to focus on and potentially negotiate in any employment arrangement. These key items are what minimally should be included in the agreement, reflected in items one through eight of Exhibit 25.1:

1. Period or term of the agreement

2. Salary and compensation

3. Paid time off

4. Employee benefits

Exhibit 25.1
Employment Agreement Considerations

1. Period/Term of the Agreement (with a specific start date)
2. Salary and Compensation (including amounts and time frames)
   a. Base salary
   b. Annual or periodic bonus
   c. Incentive program
   d. Commission structure
   e. Stock options
   f. Other compensation
   g. Overtime work and compensation
3. Paid Time Off
   a. Vacation time
   b. Sick time
   c. Other PTO
4. Employee Benefits (including what you are accepting and declining)
   a. Health insurance
   b. Life insurance
   c. Dental insurance
   d. Vision program
   e. 401k or pension plan
   f. Cafeteria plan
   g. Health club membership
5. Position Description, Grade Level, Duties, and Scope of Responsibilities
   a. Description at the time of hire
   b. How to modify the position description when promoted
   c. First project expectations and success criteria
6. Performance Evaluations, Time Periods, and Frequency
7. Performance Measurement Process
   a. Define goals and objectives
   b. Measure performance based upon your individual performance
   c. Compensation increase structure/ranges
8. Work Location (office, home office, virtual/remote)
9. Non-Compete Clause
10. Non-Solicitation Clause (of clients and employees)
11. Confidentiality Clause
12. Conflict of Interest Clause
13. Moving and Relocation Expense Reimbursement
14. Work Related Expense Reimbursement
15. Arbitration Clause
16. Company Automobile or Car Allowance
17. Company Supplied Equipment
18. Proprietary/Confidential Property and Information
19. Termination Provision
   a. Severance compensation (minimally two weeks salary for each year of employment)
   b. Financial counseling
   c. Outplacement services
20. Child Care
21. Travel Requirements and Reimbursement

5. Position description, grade level, duties, and scope of responsibilities

6. Performance evaluations, time periods, and frequency

7. Performance measurement process

8. Work location (office, home office, virtual/remote)

Key Strategies and Suggestions

Let's review some strategies and suggestions regarding the employment agreement and some of its more critical components.

General

- The job offer or employment agreement should be in writing.

- Negotiate at the time you receive the offer, never before.

- Read and understand the document thoroughly and take your time.

- Review the agreement with a lawyer, friend, or business associate.

- Minimally, review and discuss it with the hiring manager and someone from HR.

- Request from the company a reasonable amount of time to review the document, allowing you to focus on what is important to you and allowing you to compare it with other offers and opportunities.

- Everything *can* be discussed, and everything *may* be negotiable.

- Strive for an agreement that is reasonable, clear, brief, and thorough.

- Focus on what is most important to you and negotiate hard on those items. Give up items you deem not as important.

- Do not cut off other opportunities until you actually start your new job.

Compensation

- Determine what you are worth and develop a realistic compensation expectation (preferably prior to receiving an offer):
  - Review salary surveys and local/regional compensation reports.

    Note: For an extensive and broad range of compensation data, access the U.S. Bureau of Labor Statistics website at www. bls.gov. Additionally, for a diverse range of national, regional, and local salary and employment data options, simply enter "salary survey" into your favorite Internet search engine.
  - Talk to headhunters or professional staffing firms.
  - Review professional journals.
  - Review salary databases (available online and at your local library).
  - Participate in industry or job-related user groups.
  - Consult business associates and networking contacts.
  - Consider your personal financial needs and the value you believe you can add to the position and the company.

- Get as much as you can up front and define the process for getting more compensation at a later time.

- Start high. When asked, "What are you looking for?" tell them directly and be prepared to explain your justification. Suggest a number that is 10–20 percent above your minimum requirement. You can always come down, but you can never go up once you provide the employer with a number.

- Your prospective employer is ultimately targeting your salary to be at or below the median salary for the salary range defined by the company for the job grade or level, yet they probably can approve your compensation up to as much as 20 percent beyond the median or midpoint. Do whatever you can to obtain the job grade compensation details from the company.

- Your compensation should not necessarily be tied to your compensation history, unless it is to your absolute advantage.

- Your compensation should be tied to the perceived (initially) and actual value you bring to the position and the company.

- Compensation *must* be tied to personal performance as well as team/departmental/corporate goals.

- Specify the particulars of your grade level, starting salary, and promotion opportunities in as much detail as possible.

- Cash versus company stock. Take the cash in the form of a higher starting salary first, then if you can, ask for any stock options or other company stock benefits as well. You will benefit from the salary increase from the first day of your employment, while the benefits of stock options and corresponding benefits may never materialize.

Employee Benefits

- Understand the details of the standard benefits available to all employees and obtain from HR the necessary documentation for each of the benefits.

- Inquire about non-standard benefits that are offered on a discretionary basis.

- Consider the value of the benefits to you now and in the future, and pay particular attention to the employee cost of certain benefits, such as health insurance premium contributions.

- Insist on tax-deferral savings alternatives, like a company-sponsored 401(k).

Performance Evaluations, Process, and Measurement

- Work with the hiring manager to define the details of your first project and how you will be evaluated on that project and include those details in the agreement. This information can provide you with a sense of how desperately you might be needed or how critical you are to the success of the project. You can use the information to your advantage when negotiating the compensation aspect of your agreement.

- Define the specifics of how you will be evaluated overall and the criteria used to consider you for promotion opportunities and compensation increases. With this information, *you* can track and manage your progress over time.

- Plan to document your performance as you proceed with your career.

- Insist on an annual (minimally) performance and salary review.

The Non-Competition Clause

Many companies today include a variety of clauses designed to protect only the company. They will insist that these clauses are necessary and required for the finalized agreement, but that does not mean they cannot be discussed and modified. The most common of these clauses that can have an impact on your future career is the non-compete clause.

- Solidify in the agreement a clear definition of what "non-competition" really means. In general, a non-compete clause prevents you from pursuing a similar job that is in competition against your employer for a specified period of time after you leave their employment. The clause generally specifies that you cannot work for the company's competition, usually within a defined geographic region. Essentially, the clause states that if the company is going to employ you, you cannot use your experience and what you may learn to your personal advantage and at the possible expense of the company—by competing against them for business.

- Focus on reasonability. Ultimately, your employer cannot prevent you from working or pursuing a livelihood, and many states support this premise. At the same time, you need to respect the arrangement between you and your employer and define the details so they protect you both equally.

- Be sure to specify a period of time during which you are not allowed to compete. A standard and reasonable time period is twelve months from the termination of your employment. Any longer period should be negotiated along with other compensation and severance arrangements.

- Try to limit the non-compete to specific companies.

- Try to limit the non-compete to a specific geographic region.

- Try to limit the non-compete to your areas of involvement.

What If the Company Does Not Have a Formal Agreement?

It is possible that the company that you are considering does not have a standard employment agreement. Because of the company's size or its corporate culture, there may not even be a formal, written offer letter. That should not deter you from considering the opportunity. Instead, take it upon yourself to solidify and substantiate the details of your agreement.

- Draft a letter yourself, summarizing your understanding of the employment arrangement and provide it to your prospective employer.

- You can suggest that other companies you are interviewing with have a written employment agreement. Work with the company to prepare a more formal document.

- Even after you start the new job, keep everything—check stubs, benefits agreements, and statements, etc. These documents will provide a historical reference of much of what would be in the agreement.

- Get the company handbook; it can serve as a de facto employment agreement.

Questions to Ask and Topics to Cover

Back in Chapter 22 (page 172), we discussed not raising certain questions or issues until you actually receive the job offer. Well, now is that time.

Questions you may want to ask the hiring manager involve:

- promotion and career opportunities within the department;

- career-growth opportunities throughout the company;

- discussion of work schedules and travel expectations;

- whether future salary adjustments are standard for all employees or based upon performance (what are the ranges?); and,

- any negative aspects of the job you identified in your job profile.

Questions for the HR department may involve:

- promotions and career opportunities throughout the organization;

- management of vacation and sick time;

- confirmation of job grade or levels and corresponding salary ranges;

- benefits and employment-related questions;

- specific questions about the employee handbook; and,

- any negative aspects of the job you identified in your job profile.

It is appropriate to speak with both your hiring manager and a representative from HR to obtain all of the information you need to make an informed decision. Be thorough in your inquiries and do not be afraid to ask what you feel is an important question.

The Job Offer Scorecard

Once you have discussed the employment agreement with your prospective employer and have had all of your questions answered, complete a final evaluation of your offer. Throughout the interviewing and job offer process, so much can be discussed, defined, and modified, that sometimes it is difficult to remember all of the details. Additionally, I am confident that if you effectively executed *The First 60 Seconds* approach, you will have more than one job offer to consider. To evaluate the details of a particular job offer and how those details compare to another offer, it is helpful to compile the most important decision-making criteria (as defined by you) in a simple form.

Exhibit 25.2 on page 216 shows a Job Offer Scorecard that you can use to evaluate one or more offers you are considering. While the Job Offer Scorecard includes many of the recommended criteria for making a sound and rational decision, it is important that you review and modify the scorecard to accurately include those criteria that are most important to *you*.

For each offer, provide a rating for criteria based on your research, your interview, the details of your offer, and any discussions you may have had with the company. Rate each of the criteria as Below Average, Average, or Above Average. Consolidating and summarizing the details will help you step back and make a well-informed decision.

Use the Job Offer Scorecard to evaluate the job offers you are considering.

The Closing Communications

Once you have decided to accept your employment offer, there are just a few more details required to finish up your job search process.

Exhibit 25.2
Job Offer Scorecard

	Job Offer A	Job Offer B	Job Offer C
Company			
Financial Strength/Stability			
Company Outlook			
Industry Outlook			
Location			
Other: _____			
Job/Position			
Compensation (Base)			
Compensation (Bonus and Incentive)			
Grade Level			
Nature of Work			
Work Location			
Work Hours/Flexibility			
Work Environment			
Short-Term Position Growth Opportunities			
Long-Term Promotion Opportunities			
Positive Aspects of the Position			
Negative Aspects of the Position			
Other: _____			
Hiring/Direct Manager			
Management Style			
Management Philosophy			
Personal Motivations and Priorities			
Personality and Interpersonal Skills			
Employee Performance Appraisal Approach			
Can Be a Mentor?			
Other: _____			
Benefits			
Health Insurance			
Dental Insurance			
Life Insurance			
Short-Term Disability			
Long-Term Disability			
401(k) Plan			
Employee Stock Ownership Plan			
Pension Plan			
Vacation Days			
Sick Days			
Other: _____			
RATINGS: N/A - Not Applicable 1 - Below Average 2 - Average 3 - Above Average			

Of course, you first want to get back to the company whose offer you are accepting and let them know the good news. You can notify them by phone or email, but you want to immediately send the following:

- Acceptance of Offer Letter (Refer to Exhibit 25.3 on page 218 for a sample letter)—this letter can be sent in either electronic or hard-copy form, and a copy should be sent to both the hiring manager and the HR representative involved in the process.

- signed original of the employment agreement

In addition, if you have not done so already, notify any other companies that you were interviewing with that you are no longer available. (See Chapter 24; page 187.)

 Prepare and send an Acceptance of Offer Letter to the company whose offer you are accepting.

Exhibit 25.3
Acceptance of Offer Letter

Month DD, YYYY

Mr. John Smith
XYZ Corporation
1234 North Shore Drive
My Town, IL 12345-6789

Dear Mr. Smith:

Thank you very much for your offer of employment with XYZ Corporation and for your time to discuss the details of that offer.

I am pleased to accept your offer, and I am looking forward to starting work with you and your team on <u>Month, DD</u>. Attached is the executed employment agreement and corresponding documents you have requested.

I appreciate your confidence in my abilities and I look forward to being an effective and successful member of the organization.

Sincerely,

Your Name
(123) 456-7890
yourname@email.com

CHAPTER 26

Your First Day

*The first day of your new job is the
first day of the rest of your career.*

You have come a long way, and the deal is finally done—almost. The deal is not officially closed until you actually start your new job.

Do you remember what it was like on the first day of school? It didn't matter which grade or which year—they were all the same. You would come back from a nice, long summer vacation, and it was like you were starting all over again. It was a new grade with a new teacher and a new group of classmates. It was a clean slate.

The first day on a new job is very much the same as the first day back to school. In a single eight-hour day, you will experience anxiety and excitement and be confronted with many of the same challenges as that first day of school, including new people to meet, friendships to make, and new information to grasp. You have the opportunity to establish a foundation that will jump-start your new job and lay the groundwork for your future success.

Why the First Day Is So Important

You may be thinking, *What's the big deal, it's just one day and I'll have a long time to establish myself and get going.* Actually, if you have made it this far in the book I doubt you are thinking that way. We have talked a lot about differentiation and the extra effort required to set yourself apart from the crowd. We are going to apply that same line of reasoning to approaching the first day of your new job.

There are a number of reasons why the first day of your new job is so important:

- Remember that you are not done with your job search process and the deal is not closed until you actually start your new job. A lot can happen from the time you accept the job offer and your first day.

- You will have the opportunity to initiate and establish important relationships with your co-workers and other important and influential people within the organization.

- Just because you received a job offer does not mean that you will be successful at your new job. Your boss and co-workers will be assessing and evaluating you from the moment you walk in as an official employee.

- Everyone will be watching you. They have heard about you, about your background and experience, and they're wondering what you will actually be like as a member of the team. You need to show them.

It is important to view the first day as one of great opportunity for you. On your first day, you have the ability to firmly establish who you are and what your role in the organization will be. From the first moment, you have the ability to differentiate yourself and confirm with conviction that you are the best person for the job. You have the ability to establish a first and lasting impression with your co-workers and customers in a way that positively impacts the success you have in your new role.

The First 60 Seconds Revisited

The impact of the first day of your new job is also similar to the impact of the first impression you made on the day of your interview.

A decisive qualification will be made about you within the first 60 seconds from the time you meet each person on your first day at work.

Prepare for your first day of work exactly like you did for your first interview—everything applies. It would be a great idea to go back and review the entire section titled The First 60 Seconds (pages 109–144) in preparation for your first day. Some of the major highlights include:

- adequate preparation;

- being on time;

- the look (wow! yes! whew!);

- the greeting ("It is truly a pleasure to meet you."); and,

- the relationship (make a positive connection).

In the same way you initially impressed the hiring manager or interviewer at your first meeting, you want to have the same impact on the people you meet the first day on your new job—the staff and your co-workers, your boss's boss, your clients, your customers, etc.

You have one primary objective on your first day of a new job: to effectively manage the first 60 seconds of each encounter with a new person.

Position Yourself for Success

Starting on your first day, you also have the opportunity to effectively position yourself for everything you may want to do—and achieve—in the coming weeks, months, and years. The sooner you start, the sooner you will realize the benefits.

I'm talking about things you can start doing from day one, as you are meeting people and as you begin to get acclimated to your new role, responsibilities, and environment.

Focus on developing relationships.

Everyone you meet has the opportunity to positively impact your career future. A co-worker today could be your boss tomorrow. A customer today can be an even bigger customer down the road. Treat everyone you meet with dignity and respect. Most importantly, remember that you will spend a significant amount of time with your co-workers—in many cases more time than you will spend with your friends and family. Focus on developing a positive relationship with everyone you meet. Your career, and your life, will be better for it.

Identify the successful people in the department and company.

Take the time to learn about the people you meet. You will be surprised how easy it is to identify the most successful people in the organization. Determine the qualities and traits of these successful people and see if you can develop similar qualities and traits to make you a better employee. Successful people are successful for good reason—you just need to take the time to think about what makes them different, then try to model those behaviors.

Identify influential people in the organization, including senior management, internal customers, and external customers.

As quickly as you can, identify key and influential people within the organization. Inquire with your co-workers and obtain and review available organizational charts. Your objective is to know by name, title, and responsibility all of the key people within the organization. With this knowledge you will be well prepared for when you first meet these people or have the opportunity to work with them. You also will know the people you ultimately want to work and be associated with.

"Bring It On!"

Early in my career I identified a very easy way to differentiate myself from just about anyone else.

I said "yes" when most others said "no."

From my first job, I noticed a common pattern of the typical worker. Once job responsibilities were defined and determined for a person, there seemed to be a reluctance to change them. Over many years, I saw time and time again where a person was given an opportunity to take on an additional challenge or responsibility, only to see that person decline. It could have been for any one of a thousand different reasons, but the point was clear to me: most of my co-workers did not openly or proactively make the effort to take on additional work or responsibility. People became comfortable with their daily routine and just did not want to change it.

And I saw it as a great opportunity.

I started saying, "Yes!"—for everything.

My manager would ask our team if anyone had some free time to take on an additional project, and I said, "Yes!" A customer would call and ask if I could help solve a problem, and I said, "Yes!" There were even situations where a manager or customer would ask if I had experience in something-or-the-other, and would I be interested in taking on a similar challenge, and I said, "Yes!"

I quickly found that the response from management and customers was extremely positive. They had a problem and needed someone to help them and I was that person. With a single question, and in that single momentary response, they had a solution to their problem. They were happy.

Now you have to understand, most of time I really did not have the extra available time and in many cases I did not have the exact (or any) experience necessary to take on the additional challenge. But that did not concern me. By saying, "Yes!" I was exposing myself to a world of opportunities that I otherwise wouldn't have had. I learned things beyond my wildest expectations.

And you know what else happened? Very quickly after delivering successfully on the first couple of tasks, management would see that I had a lot on my plate and decided that I could use some assistance. They would come to me with a new challenge and would also give me resources to do the work. In short order, the number of different opportunities I was exposed to increased significantly and the ability to learn new things was nurtured and supported. They ended up helping me to help them. They were happy and I was happy.

So on your first day especially, and also after that, take on as much responsibility as you can possibly muster, and then take on some more. Don't worry about how you are going to deliver on that responsibility until you actually have it. Once the responsibility is yours, you will find that options and solutions will come to you like never before—from your own devices and from those people around you. You will also find that your manager will give you the opportunity to figure it out and will support you in your endeavors.

When your manager and customers see you as a problem solver and a person who delivers, you will find that many other things will happen as well. If you are so inclined, your leadership and management opportunities will expand, as will the number of people you are responsible for. Your performance and salary reviews will be much more positive, and you will have an easier time justifying how you exceeded the expectations of your job. You will find promotion opportunities presented to you more frequently and before anyone else, and in the unfortunate situation when a company has to cut back on staff, you will be the last considered. No matter how bad it might get at a company, they are not going to let their go-to person get away, especially if you are responsible for the most critical projects.

Consider the "bring it on" mentality. It is a simple and effective differentiator with immediate and broad-sweeping benefits to job success and to the future growth and development of your career.

Consider it simply because no one else will.

🕐 *Bring It On!* Say "yes" when others say "no."

The End and the Beginning

And so we come to the end of your job search process. You have successfully managed and executed *The First 60 Seconds* approach and you have obtained that next great career opportunity. Your first day is behind you and you have a great future ahead of you.

So let's start planning for your next career opportunity.

Section 5

Your 60-Month Career Plan

The point of the journey is not to arrive; anything can happen...
—*Neil Peart*

CHAPTER 27

The Future Begins Now

Whether you are embarking on the first job of your career or your tenth, it's easy to become content with your recent accomplishment. After all, you have worked hard to get this great opportunity, and it's reasonable to think that your career management efforts are done for the time being. I'll give you that. Take a week or two, celebrate your new position, and get acclimated to your new job responsibilities and the expectations of your new employer. Then let's get back to work, *for the future begins now*.

With your first job, and with each subsequent career opportunity you may acquire, you are making one stop on your career journey. It is one destination in your long-term plan, in which you have made a substantial financial and personal investment. Getting to your next destination—your next career opportunity—is a journey, one of excitement, challenge, and determination. But once at your destination, you must continue on. You must develop the itinerary for traveling to the next stop on your journey.

Career planning and management has to be a continual and evolving process. In the same way that you invested the necessary time and resources to develop and differentiate yourself to secure your new career opportunity, you need to make that same commitment to future career plans. By making the commitment now, and by focusing on continuous incremental improvement and continuous career planning, you maintain your ability to differentiate yourself from the competition and will realize your long-term career goal more efficiently and with greater associated benefits.

🕐 **Commit to continual and incremental career planning and improvement.**

A commitment to continually plan and manage your career does not have to require a significant amount of effort, but it does require effort. With a small amount of up front effort and regularly scheduled checkpoints, you will do more to manage your career than almost anyone else. You will be in complete control of your career and financial success.

Setting Expectations for Your Future

If you have not done so already, start planning for your next career opportunity and your long-term career goal. As you proceed with this chapter and complete the goal setting and planning activities, it is important that you set *appropriate and realistic* expectations for yourself.

You need to know where you are going and how you plan to get there.

Not having a specific career goal and a corresponding plan is like driving in unfamiliar territory without a destination and without a map and directions. Where *are* you going? What is the best route to get there? Will you know the detours and distractions (and attractions) when you see them and how will you react to them? Without a goal and a plan, you're driving blind. Before you embark on your next journey, take the time to define your destination and the road you will take to get there.

Only you can look out for your own best interests.

Maybe you have the greatest boss or manager in the world. Maybe you have a mentor within the industry who has taken you under his or her wing to educate and guide you. Or maybe you have neither. Regardless, never assume that anyone else will be looking out for your best career interests. The only person you can count on, day in and day out, to absolutely ensure that you meet your career goals, is *you*. You must take charge of managing your career, and you have to start today.

If you're comfortable, you're finished.

The day you become comfortable in your current job position is the day that your long-term career goal is in jeopardy. You cannot afford to let this happen. If it does happen, you need to take immediate action to kick your career management efforts into high gear. While comfort and stability in your current position may seem like a good thing, there are way too many negative repercussions that can sneak up on you. These can include loss of job satisfaction, mediocre performance and compensation appraisals, and the loss of your job. If you are serious about pursuing a successful long-term career, you must be serious about future career growth and the financial rewards and benefits that come with that growth. Being comfortable in your job will not allow you to pursue that successful career direction.

Follow the rule of compounding interest.

Think about how compounding interest benefits you and your bank account. Your bank computes interest on the balance you have in your account and adds that interest to your account balance. Assuming you have not withdrawn any funds from the account, the next time the interest is computed, your account balance is higher and subsequently the new amount of computed interest is higher.

The same holds true with respect to your compensation. At your next compensation review, your manager will determine the increase you should get by applying an increase percentage to your current base salary and will add that increase amount to determine what your new salary will be. The better you are able to meet and exceed your employer's job expectations and the sooner you can get and maximize your next compensation increase, the more effective you will be at compounding your compensation increases (your interest) and realizing greater long-term financial success.

Take into account the rule of compounding interest to manage your long-term compensation growth.

Follow the ten-for-ten rule.

The ten-for-ten rule is a premise for managing your career that suggests that a 10 percent additional effort on your part—above what is required of you in your current role—will put you in the top 10 percent of your competition in your organization and industry. The reason is that most people tend to focus on doing only what is expected of them. If you were to assume that there were no underperformers within the workplace (which is unrealistic) and that everyone met expectations, then everyone would be the same—the norm. You want to be different. Take this additional 10 percent effort into consideration, and you can develop a more aggressive (and yet still realistic) career goal and plan.

Implement the ten-for-ten rule into your career planning efforts.

The 60-Month Career Plan

The 60-Month Career Plan outlines a comprehensive plan for helping you meet your long-term career goal over the next five years. The 60-Month Career Plan is designed to satisfy the following objectives:

- Maximize return (career and compensation growth) with minimal relative investment.

- Assist in defining specific and realistic short- and long-term career goals that are easy to prepare and understand, and that can be easily modified and updated over time as you track your progress.

- Guide you in using *The First 60 Seconds* skills you have acquired in an ongoing and continual fashion.

Given the theme throughout the book so far, can you guess how many minutes per month I will suggest that you invest in your career planning and management activities? If you guessed 60 minutes, you're right on the mark. The 60-Month Career Plan is structured so that it will require just 60 minutes per month—every month—to effectively manage your goals and plans. Can you afford to invest just one hour of your time every month—twelve hours a year—to take complete control of your career future? Sure you can, especially when you come to understand the benefits.

Your 60-Month Career Plan

The 60-Month Career Plan is a four-step iterative and continuous process for managing your career.

Step One: Develop and Review Your Career Goals and Plan

The first step is to define a specific and realistic goal for you to achieve within a 60-month period. Your goal setting activities will press you to be aggressive with your 60-Month Goal and will suggest that you set your expectations high. With the 60-Month Goal in place, you will then define one-year goals and corresponding plans that support your 60-Month Goal.

60-Month Goal Setting

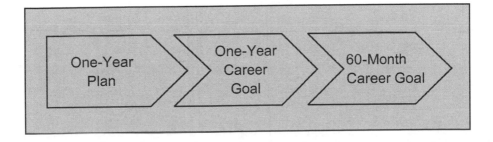

Step Two: Prospecting Career Growth Opportunities

With your plans in place, prospect for those opportunities that will help you achieve your goal. We will cover a variety of strategies for identifying and evaluating career opportunities within your current organization as well as opportunities within your industry and beyond. You will find that if you know where to look, there can be endless opportunities for you to consider.

Step Three: Preparing for Your Next Career

Once you have started prospecting for available opportunities that might be suitable for you, it is time to start preparing for that next career opportunity. This step will focus on two primary activities: (1) regularly updating your Professional Experience Inventory and related documentation, and (2) developing a plan for continuous, incremental learning and personal development. You can never be sure when that next great career opportunity will present itself, and you must be ready when it does. Additionally, by making the extra effort to improve, you will uncover opportunities you may never have thought possible. In fact, you will find that you can create many opportunities yourself through your incremental learning and personal development efforts.

Step Four: The First 60 Seconds for Life

The last step of the 60-Month Career Plan focuses on *The First 60 Seconds*, and how to effectively use the strategies and techniques in other career and life situations. You will find that just as the interviewer makes a decisive qualification of you within the first 60 seconds from the time you meet, other people in your profession and in your life are making similar 60-second qualifications.

Start Planning Today for the Rest of Your Life

It is important to note that the first three steps outlined above are to be completed in succession, as the results of one step have a direct impact on the activities of the next step. And remember that the process is iterative, so as you complete the three steps, you return to and review step one. For the fourth step—*The First 60 Seconds* for Life—while it will be part of your monthly review process, I suggest that you make every effort to implement this step as part of your daily life.

The future is in your hands. Everything you do, every additional effort you make from this point forward, will have a direct impact on the future success of your career. With a minimal investment on your part to more proactively manage your career, you will stay one step ahead of everyone else and realize your career goals on your terms.

Remember to focus on small and incremental activities and improvement, and do them on a continual, iterative basis.

 Continual planning, learning, preparation, differentiation, and taking advantage of every *First 60 Seconds* encounter that may arise will put *you* in complete control of *your* career.

CHAPTER 28

Goals and Plans

Where Are You Going and How Are You Going to Get There?

No matter how simple or brief, a defined set of goals and corresponding plans are of paramount importance if you want to achieve success, satisfy your career objectives, and ultimately satisfy your personal wants and needs.

Too often, it's easy to get comfortable with your present career role. But stay alert; getting too comfortable can lead to serious trouble. On the one hand, if you have a set of goals and corresponding plans to meet those goals, and you are managing your plans effectively, then you have every reason to feel comfortable and content. However, if you are just riding out each day at work doing the minimum required and collecting a paycheck, and have no plan for how you are going to progress to the next level of your career, you're asking for trouble. If you have no aspirations for growing and advancing in your career, then you do not need a goal or a plan, but realize that you will have to be content with *everything* staying exactly as it is. But as I have mentioned before, if you have made it to this point, I know that you are not like that.

> To be successful in your career, you need some kind of formal long- and short-term goals and plans to help you realize those goals.

Ask friends, family, and business associates—ask as many people as you can if they have any type of career goal and a corresponding plan for meeting that goal. Ask those who do have a goal and a plan if it is written down and how often they review it to see if they are on track. I think you might be surprised at the responses you get. Or maybe you can guess at what the results will be. The reality is, many individuals do not have any goals set and do not have a written career plan to help them realize their career objectives. It looks to me like we have just stumbled on another very easy way to differentiate yourself from just about everyone else in your company or industry.

Develop a written set of career goals and plans.

Goal setting should not be a time-consuming activity. While you can invest as much time as you want, I suggest starting with a simple and time-manageable approach that you can implement and stick to. Developing extensive goals and plans that end up in the back of your desk never to be seen again misses the mark. Any plan, no matter how simple, that you can consistently review and manage on a regular basis, will be beneficial.

> Remember: Any goal you set or plan you prepare—*in writing*—no matter how simple, will be more than what just about anyone else has done. That's differentiation!

As we proceed with this chapter, we will cover several topics and discuss several activities you can easily follow and implement to make your goal setting and planning more successful. In doing so, our objectives will be as follows:

- Achieve maximum return with minimal investment.

- Understand your wants and needs.

- Define long- and short-term goals.

- Prepare simple and straightforward plans that are easy to follow, update, and manage.

- Commit to review and update your plan on a regularly scheduled basis: once every month.

A Framework for Goal Setting and Planning

As you prepare your goals and plans, keep in mind that each component is just one part of your overall approach. Each component that we address throughout this chapter will be independent in its focus and objective but will have a significant impact on other components in the framework.

Refer to Exhibit 28.1, which provides the 60-Month Goal Planning Timeline, for the framework you should refer back to regularly as you proceed with goal setting and planning.

Points to note:

- Your One-Year and 60-Month (Five-Year) Goals are fully integrated, and the shorter-term goals must support the longer-term goal. Each of your One-Year Goals must directly support and help lead to the achievement of your 60-Month Goal.

- Each of your One-Year Plans will directly support each of your One-Year Goals and will subsequently support the realization of your 60-Month Goal.

- It is important that you formally document the success of each One-Year Plan after the year is over so that you can make any necessary modifications to your remaining goals and plans.

Developing a Set of Goals

What is a goal?

As it relates to your career, your goal will be a specific, defined, and formal (written) description of the end result you wish to achieve. You follow that up with the detailed plans outlining the effort you will put forth to reach that goal.

Exhibit 28.1
60-Month Goal Planning Timeline

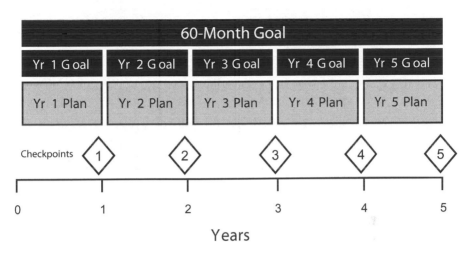

The level of effort put forth has a direct and positive impact on your ability to achieve your goal, with two caveats. First, your efforts must be focused and well managed in order to be effective. Second, do not confuse activity with focused effort. Just putting in the hours without regard to a specific goal and plan will produce little discernable benefit.

What is it that you want to achieve and why? That can be a difficult question to answer, but it is worth spending time to think about and come up with one or more things to consider and formalize. Aside from forcing you to get up in the morning, is there any reason why you go to work?

Goals can take many forms and can cover many disparate areas. For this discussion, goals can basically be categorized into two major segments:

1. Life supporting and sustaining (needs)

- food

- shelter

- basic life necessities

2. Life enhancing (wants)

- acquisition of physical things

- personal and social development

- building wealth

These are very broad categories, so within each are dozens of different subcategories that might be important to you. As you proceed with your goal setting, define your life-sustaining goals first and follow with realistic plans to meet those basic needs. With your basic needs addressed, then you set goals and plans for additional things you may want.

Your goal can be anything at all. The only requirement is that you believe in it, be passionate about it, and have a strong desire to achieve it.

It is important to *define long- and short-term goals*. Your long-term goal can be loftier. Be aggressive and set a goal beyond what you think might be realistic. Your shorter-term goals should provide more immediate and measurable results that, while providing benefit now, will also help you achieve your long-term goal.

You can easily define your goals by following a simple five-step goal setting process:

1. Determine your wants and needs.

2. Define your 60-Month Goal.

3. Define your one-year goals.

4. Develop your one-year plan.

5. Schedule and implement a 60-Minutes-Per-Month Checkup regimen.

 Follow and implement the five-step goal setting process.

Let's get started.

Step One: Determining Your Needs and Wants

Start with a quick exercise to assist in determining what is most important to you. It is extremely difficult to define a goal if you have no idea of what you need and want in life.

- What motivates you?

- Why are you working?

- What do you want and need, for yourself and your family?

Please refer to the Need and Wants Worksheet in Exhibit 28.2 on page 240.

The worksheet provides a straightforward guide for helping formally define your needs and wants. The form is self-explanatory and the only requirement is that you fill out the worksheet as thoroughly as possible. This is an opportunity to brainstorm write down everything that comes to mind. If you think it's a good idea or is important, write it down. There are no wrong answers. Your objective is to get as much down on paper as you can. Use multiple sheets to provide an exhaustive list of what you want and need for yourself and your family.

Set aside some time to complete this exercise before proceeding to Step Two.

> Remember: It is better to have more than less. You will benefit from having more to consider, and you can always pare it down later if you feel it necessary.

Step Two: Defining Your 60-Month Goal

Now that you have written down all of your specific needs and wants, it is time to review and evaluate them, and turn them into a specific long-term goal.

This will likely be the most challenging part of the five-step goal setting process. Step Two requires the most thought and challenges you to be brave enough to define an aggressive and lofty goal for you to strive for in a 60-month period.

Exhibit 28.2
Needs and Wants Worksheet

Identify the top three reasons why you work or what you expect to accomplish from
your work:

1.
2.
3.

NEEDS

Identify the Basic *NEEDS* You Must Satisfy: <u>Immediate</u>   <u>In 1 Year</u>   <u>In 5 Years</u>

1. _____   ☐   ☐   ☐
2. _____   ☐   ☐   ☐
3. _____   ☐   ☐   ☐
4. _____   ☐   ☐   ☐
5. _____   ☐   ☐   ☐

For one or all of the Basic *NEEDS* identified, specify why they are important to you.

1. _____
2. _____
3. _____
4. _____
5. _____

WANTS

Identify Those *WANTS* That Will Improve
or Enhance Your Life: <u>Immediate</u>   <u>In 1 Year</u>   <u>In 5 Years</u>

1. _____   ☐   ☐   ☐
2. _____   ☐   ☐   ☐
3. _____   ☐   ☐   ☐
4. _____   ☐   ☐   ☐
5. _____   ☐   ☐   ☐

For one or all of your *WANTS* identified, specify why they are important to you.

1. _____
2. _____
3. _____
4. _____
5. _____

First, review your Needs and Wants Worksheet and identify which ones are essential or most important to you. Then think about the financial requirements necessary to support your wants and needs. Based upon your financial requirements, where does your career need to be in order to support those financial requirements—now and in the future? Aside from financial requirements, are there other requirements that must be fulfilled?

Once you've thought it through, prepare a Goals Worksheet like the one provided in Exhibit 28.3 on page 242. Write down your 60-Month Goal in as much detail as possible. Then, write down why that goal is important to you, specifically relating to the most important needs and wants the goal satisfies. If your goal has meaning and is important to you, you'll be able to develop passion and conviction to work toward that goal.

Note: Do not worry too much about defining the "perfect" 60-Month Goal. You can adjust once you have developed your five one-year goals in the next step.

Step Three: Defining Your One-Year Goals

In this step, you dissect your long term 60 Month Goal into five smaller, more manageable, and more easily achievable one-year goals. This is where some magic happens, helping you realize the following.

It is easy to reach a larger goal by breaking it up into smaller pieces.

Each of the one-year goals will be only one-fifth as difficult to achieve as opposed to addressing the 60-Month Goal as one big effort.

After you define each of your five individual one-year goals, you may realize that your 60-Month Goal is not challenging, aggressive, or lofty enough. You will realize that if you can achieve your goals on an annual basis, you can realize incredible long-term career growth, success, personal improvement, and the financial rewards that come with all of those.

Take time now to write down a goal for each of the next five years that will support your efforts to realize your 60-Month Goal. State why each of your goals is important to you in as much detail as possible. Again, specify the needs and wants as identified in your Needs and Wants Worksheet that your goal will satisfy.

Exhibit 28.3
Goals Worksheet

60-Month Goal for the Target Year _____ :

Statement of Goal and Why This Is Important to Me

_____

_____

_____

Year One Goal for the Target Year _____ :

Statement of Goal and Why This Is Important to Me

_____

_____

_____

Year Two Goal for the Target Year _____ :

Statement of Goal and Why This Is Important to Me

_____

_____

_____

Year Three Goal for the Target Year _____ :

Statement of Goal and Why This Is Important to Me

_____

_____

_____

Year Four Goal for the Target Year _____ :

Statement of Goal Here and Why This Is Important to Me

_____

_____

_____

Year Five Goal for the Target Year _____ :

Statement of Goal Here and Why This Is Important to Me

_____

_____

_____

Step Four: Developing Your One-Year Plan

With your goals defined, the next step is to develop the plans necessary to help you reach those goals. Planning can sometimes be an insurmountable effort, which is why many people never do it, whether it is for their career or for anything else. I will make the planning process a straightforward and hopefully enjoyable process for you.

To keep things simple, for now just focus on developing a plan for the first year. Refer to Exhibit 28.4 on page 244 for a template you can use. For this and any other one-year plans you develop, focus on and include the following:

- Restate your five- and one-year goals.

- Identify the specific career activities you need to complete and expectations you need to satisfy to accomplish your one-year goal.

- Identify the specific personal development activities you need to complete to accomplish your goal.

- Review the Ongoing Areas of Focus section and incorporate these and other related activities into your plan.

Take the time now to complete the plan for year one.

Step Five: 60 Minutes per Month Checkup

As I mentioned in the beginning of the chapter, preparing your goals and plans only to have them disappear forever in your desk does no good. You have made the initial investment; now all you have to do is follow that up with a little ongoing maintenance to make sure you stay on track.

Commit to spending just 60 minutes each month—just twelve hours out of an entire year—to review, maintain, and manage your goals and plans and to achieve the career success you deserve. Here's how the 60-Minute Checkup should work:

Exhibit 28.4
One-Year Plan Worksheet

<u>One-Year Plan for the Year 2XXX</u>

60-Month Goal for the Target Year 2XXX:

Statement of Goal Here

Year X (Year one through five) Goal:

Statement of Goal Here

Career Activities to Complete to Accomplish Goal: <u>Completed</u>

1. _____   ☐
2. _____   ☐
3. _____   ☐
4. _____   ☐
5. _____   ☐

Personal Development Activities to Complete to Accomplish Goal: <u>Completed</u>

1. _____   ☐
2. _____   ☐
3. _____   ☐
4. _____   ☐
5. _____   ☐

Ongoing Areas of Focus:

1. Be proactive in managing and planning for your career growth–*invest just one hour each month.*

2. Effectively manage every *First 60 Seconds* encounter you have with each new person you meet.

3. Continually differentiate yourself.

4. Continually say "yes" when everyone else is saying "no."

One-Year Review Comments:

_____

_____

- Perform a broad review of all goals and plans.

- Review in detail your one-year plan. Identify accomplishments. Note activities that are behind schedule and modify your plan as necessary to complete those activities within your one-year time period.

- Review and update your Professional Experience Inventory, References Summary, and Personal Profile (as defined and completed in Section I).

- Consider this: Are you effectively managing each *First 60 Seconds* encounter you have with each new person you meet? Are you continuing to differentiate yourself? Are you saying "yes" when everyone else is saying "no?"

Set your monthly check-up process on autopilot. Make a note now in your desktop or electronic calendar to remind you to complete the checkup on a regular basis.

Implement a 60 Minutes per Month Checkup regimen.

Now Go Make It Happen!

By completing the activities outlined in this chapter, you have made substantial, additional progress in differentiating yourself from your competition. You have a written set of goals and a plan for accomplishing those goals. You can be confident that you are but one of a few who have made the effort to do this. By referring to and managing your plan on a regular basis, you will achieve great success—certainly more than if you had no plan at all.

What you can ultimately accomplish is within your complete control.

Now go make it happen!

CHAPTER 29

Prospecting for Career Growth and Opportunity

What if I told you that this chapter provided you the tools and the map to find gold? What if I told you that with a little digging and a little extra effort, you could accomplish greater financial and career success—would you be interested?

Prospecting for your next career opportunity is much like digging for gold, yet with a much higher success rate. You'll find valuable career nuggets are out there, just waiting for you to take them. Prospecting can be exciting, challenging, and if you do it effectively, it can almost always provide a treasure. Opportunities to grow and further develop your career are everywhere. You don't necessarily need to look for them, as in many cases they are right there in front of you. All you need are the tools to unearth them, along with a little determination and conviction, and you will be well on your way to mining career gold.

Six Key Career Growth Strategies

There are six key strategies to identify a wealth of potential career opportunities. These strategies can also help you achieve the career and personal goals you have set. Each key strategy—networking, internal opportunities, industry opportunities, other external opportunities, mentoring, and model successful behavior—can provide numerous job and career influences and opportunities. They are not only readily available to you—they're extremely easy to take advantage of.

Implement the six key career growth strategies to effectively prospect for your next career opportunity.

The only roadblock to benefiting from any one of them is *you*. When you take yourself out of the way, and make a commitment to incorporating one or more of these strategies into your career management efforts (even in a small way), the benefits will far exceed your investment and your expectations.

Career Prospecting Strategies

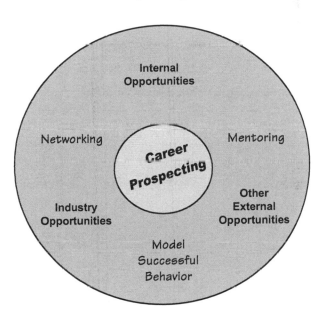

1. Networking

Meet and interact in professional and social situations to learn about other people and the opportunities they expose.

In the past, when someone told me about a networking opportunity, several thoughts raced through my mind, and to be truthful, they were not necessarily positive. I viewed networking as simply a social activity to meet people who may or may not have anything in common. I was busy at work, my social life was fine, and I felt I did not need to waste any time "networking."

Then one day a lightbulb went off in my head.

Like I did, you might be asking, why do I need to network? There is a very simple and direct answer: *you need to network because you will find* the person *who is going to give you (or refer you to) your next career opportunity.*

No matter what you may do yourself to develop your career, ultimately there is always another person standing in the way. There will always be another person making the decision to give you that next job, promotion, or business opportunity—or for those of you starting or managing your own business venture, there will be the banker, supplier, and customer potentially standing in your way. Meet and interact with other people and your options for reaching and exceeding your career goals increase. The next person you meet may know someone who has the perfect job opening or might work at a company in your industry that you have always dreamed about working for. Forgo the opportunity to network, and you end up putting the roadblocks in the path to your success.

I like to think of networking in the broadest sense of the word. It is an opportunity to meet and interact with other people who can help me or who I can benefit from. That can happen just about anywhere: within your current organization, at a restaurant or bar, at an industry seminar, at a school event for one of your children, or even walking down the street. Every person you meet provides a networking opportunity, and you can control the extent and benefit of that opportunity. And it does not have to be a one-way street. You can help and be a benefit to others as well.

We discussed earlier in the book the importance of *the relationship.* Your career success, no matter what line of work or service you pursue, is directly impacted by the people you meet and the relationships you develop. Every person you meet provides a networking opportunity of sorts, or provides a *First 60 Seconds* encounter and the opportunity to make a great first impression. Relationships not only positively impact and improve your career, they improve the quality of your life. Seek out the opportunity to meet and interact with people and develop positive and meaningful relationships. It will be worth your time.

Three Maxims of Networking

- Always take advantage of an opportunity to meet someone new

- Always take the opportunity to make a great first impression. (Remember, it all happens in 60 seconds!)

- Networking can be social, and socializing can be networking, and it can always be career-related (that is your goal). At the next gathering of an industry work group, you can socialize on a personal and professional level, and at the next birthday party for your neighbor's child you can do the same. Work is such an important part of every person's life that it will always be present in both formal networking and social situations.

Networking Success Criteria

Just by participating in the act of networking, over time you will benefit. There are a few simple points to follow to help ensure the success of your networking activities:

- *Get out there.* Real, effective networking happens in face-to-face situations with other people. Get out from behind your desk, get out of your house, and go meet someone.

- *Look outside the box.* Make an effort to meet people outside your scope of experience, involvement, and comfort zone.

- *Networking is like interviewing.* Make a great first impression. That means you will effectively manage the first 60 seconds of each meeting.
    - Make a great second impression.
    - Focus on differentiation.

- Develop a relationship.
- Always follow up in an expedient and professional manner.

2. Internal Opportunities

> Career growth opportunities are within the entire organization where you currently work.

Once you have made the decision to include networking as a component of your future career management activities, the next challenge to address is where to start. There are many opportunities for you to consider, but focus on those opportunities within your current organization first.

Why focus on internal opportunities? Simply put, making a career change within your current organization is easier, faster, and less disruptive.

- You have experience at your current company that management has seen and can quantify and relate to.

- Your employer has invested in your success and they will continue to invest in you to keep you challenged and happy, and to keep you with the organization.

- It is costly and disruptive for your employer to lose a valued employee.

- It is disruptive for you to change employers and work locations.

Prospecting for new career opportunities internally does require effort on your part; in most cases, the opportunities do not magically come to you. Instead, like all of your networking activities, take a proactive approach. Seek out and explore these opportunities. Because organizations want employees to remain with the organization, they tend to provide numerous opportunities for meeting people and exploring new relationships and career opportunities.

Where to prospect internally:

- Review company job postings on a regular basis to learn about the types of opportunities potentially available.

- Take your boss out to lunch. It's easier to develop a more personal relationship outside of the work environment. Your boss may expose you to other happenings and opportunities within your department and within the organization.

- Participate in company-sponsored extracurricular activities. Golf outings, team sports, and holiday events are all good examples.

- Join internal user groups, such as the group your company started for everyone using your desktop publishing software.

- Read the company newsletter and view the company website on a regular basis to keep abreast of the people and happenings within the company. It can provide a wealth of contact information and reveal areas within the company that may be of interest to you.

- Participate in charitable fundraising activities and company-sponsored volunteer activities, especially those championed by senior management.

Note: Participation in charitable and volunteer activities is looked at *very favorably* in most organizations, especially by management. That means not only will these events provide self-gratification, but it will be well-received by your current employer. Your next employer will also look at those events favorably, should you decide to change jobs.

You will note that only the first item mentioned—review company job boards—is specifically related to a job search activity. The rest focus on getting involved in activities that allow you to meet and develop relationships with other people. A new person you meet today could very well connect you to the next great career opportunity tomorrow.

3. Industry Opportunities

> Look for career growth opportunities outside your current organization but within your current area of expertise.

After you have explored options within your current organization, you may want to explore other opportunities outside of the organization. Your first challenge is to find those companies that are most in line with your experience and skill set. There are many ways to approach this, including industry and company research you can do both online and at your local library.

To make your efforts most effective, use prospecting strategies that expose you to the most companies and opportunities relative to your industry and experience, with the most effective use of your time.

- Register with an online job search service that allows you to post your credentials for review by interested employers, and can also provide a wealth of industry, educational, and job search information.

- Register with several professional staffing firms that specialize in working with companies within your industry.

- Seek membership with and participate in industry trade organizations.

- Subscribe to leading industry trade periodicals.

- Attend industry-sponsored career fairs and those sponsored by individual companies in your industry you may be interested in working for.

- Participate in those support groups specific to your industry, type of business, or area of specialization that provide additional educational, networking, and support forums for the benefit of the group. These groups are also formed for particular software products or business solutions you may have experience with and can be aligned with a particular skill set or job position.

4. Other External Opportunities

Look for career opportunities outside your current organization or industry.

While it may be easier to search for new career opportunities within your current organization or industry, do not discount the possibility of finding opportunities outside of those boundaries.

With a little bit of creativity, desire, effort, and perseverance, you can use your educational background and prior work experience to do just about anything you feel might be interesting and exciting.

Remember that companies (and hiring managers) hire people—people who they like and enjoy being around. With your proficiency in implementing *The First 60 Seconds* approach, along with your strong interpersonal skills, diverse educational background, and whatever work experience you may have, you can create your next career opportunity exactly how you want it, and it can be completely different from what you are doing right now.

Do you have an accounting background and want to use that and other business education and experience to launch your own business? Go for it. Do you have a general liberal arts degree yet want to pursue an area of specialization at a company you always dreamed of working for? Companies appreciate a well-rounded background and are often willing to train new employees for specialized positions. Are there new skills you acquired in your current job that might take you in a completely different career direction? All of these options and more are right there in front of you to consider.

I was fortunate to use my computer science degree and MBA degree to pursue many different career passions. I worked as a computer programmer, a systems analyst, an information technology manager, an information technology consulting business owner, a hotel owner, a real estate investor and developer, and now a writer. Take the skills and experience you have acquired and pursue your passions and interests.

> If you do what you love and truly love what you do, you will never work a day in your life.

5. Mentoring

> Learn and obtain guidance from a more experienced person in your organization, industry, or beyond.

Find a Mentor!

You might say, "That's easier said than done!" While you might be correct, it is really not that difficult to find a mentor and start benefiting from that relationship. A mentor can be found in many places, but the best place to start looking is within your current organization.

I have been lucky enough to have more than one mentor (so far) to teach and guide me through my various careers. Two of my mentors were successful managers at the first company I worked for. The relationships started as your typical manager-employee sort, but changed over time:

- Early on, I respected them as successful leaders and managers within the organization.

- I was able to show them the actual and proven results of my work.

- We developed friendships.

- I asked them for their help, responded to their efforts to help me, and showed them my commitment to my personal improvement.

Mentors are successful people and like to associate with other successful people. They also really do enjoy teaching and helping *other successful people*. You will notice I said *successful people*. Any individual interested in serving as a mentor to another person is not going to invest time and energy on just anyone. They have to see or feel something in you that makes them think you have potential.

- *Show what you've got.* Do your job, do it well, and strive to exceed expectations. Do that, and you will get noticed. Get noticed, and you have the potential to be discovered by your next mentor candidate.

- *Identify successful, more experienced people.* See "Model Successful Behavior" below.

- *Tell a prospective mentor you want to learn from his or her experience.* Say something like the following, and it is unlikely that anyone could turn you down: "I want to improve myself and my career, and I really think I could learn and benefit from your success and experience."

- *Make a commitment.* A mentor will only remain a mentor if they believe you are committed to learning and developing from their experience. Show your commitment on a regular basis.

- *Develop a relationship.* Mentoring, like business and like life, is all about relationships. You need to develop a relationship based on trust, respect, and friendship if you want it to work.

- *Make it a win-win situation.* Both the mentor and the person being mentored have to benefit from the relationship. For you, the one being mentored, that is easy. You get the benefit of the other person's experience, knowledge, and relationships they have. The mentor needs to see that you are benefiting from their experience. Make it evident, and make the mentor look good in the process.

6. Model Successful Behavior

Learn from the proven, successful behavior of others.

Each day of our lives we are in a school of sorts. Each and every day, we are exposed to people—our teachers—in a variety of encounters and situations. Every person you meet or observe has something to teach you—right or wrong. The only question for you: are you open to learning from these teachers?

In life, and specifically in your business environment, there are innumerable people doing things "right" and whose careers are benefiting from those actions. As you prospect future career opportunities, your job is to identify those people in your area of interest and learn from what they are doing on a daily basis to be successful.

You will also come across many people who seem to be better at doing the "wrong" things and whose careers are stagnant as a result. You can learn from these people as well.

- Identify successful individuals based on their accomplishments, career progression, and overall success.

- Identify the person's most proficient business-specific skills.

- Identify the interpersonal skills the person uses most effectively.

- Watch how the person interacts with others.

- Seek out these people and develop a professional working relationship and potentially a personal relationship.

- Prepare a list of behavior changes you can easily and effectively implement for yourself.

- And remember: *do not do* what has proven to be unsuccessful for others.

Make the Effort and Make Your Career

Searching for your next career opportunity takes effort. Your career growth and success is in your hands alone. Only you have your best interests in mind at all times and only you have the opportunity to make things happen consistently. Take charge of your future, and never assume that anyone else will get you that next great career opportunity.

You have all of the tools you need to identify opportunities and pursue your career goals and dreams. Most of these tools are part of you inherently and allow you to effectively develop relationships with other people. The relationships you develop in your career and in your life will provide you the greatest number or future career opportunities. Only the level of effort you wish to put forward limits the number of options for meeting and interacting with people who can enhance and improve your career. So make the effort and make your career!

CHAPTER 30

Preparing Yourself for Your Next Career Opportunity

As you think about the next stage of your career, one thing must be certain: you must be better now than you were when you first obtained the position you currently hold. You must be better in one or more aspects, including overall knowledge, experience, maturity, career-specific business and technical skills, interpersonal skills, attitude, confidence, and overall personal development.

The next person you interview with and the person who ultimately provides your next career opportunity wants to see a progression of overall growth in you. The more profound and diverse the growth you can show with respect to your career *and* personal development, the greater the chance for more exciting and challenging opportunities and the corresponding financial rewards that come with those opportunities.

Two categories of activities have a direct impact on the overall success of your career:

1. activities during the normal work day that allow you to meet and exceed the expectations of your position or role; and,

2. continuous learning activities outside of the normal work day you pursue to grow and expand your personal and career growth.

I assume that you work hard and do everything you can to meet and exceed the expectations of your current role and position. I will even assume that your co-workers are doing the same. Since we have been focusing on differentiation, in this chapter we'll discuss other development activities that can truly allow you to differentiate yourself from everyone else and get you on a fast track for personal growth and development.

Take a moment to refer to Exhibit 30.1. The chart shows by the dotted line how an investment in the activities necessary to exceed your job expectations can have a positive impact on your overall career success. These are the activities that most everyone tries to focus on as they progress through their careers. Now look at the solid line, which represents an investment in the activities necessary to exceed your job expectations *and* the implementation of a continuous learning regimen. *By focusing on continuous learning, you can have a dramatic, profound, and positive impact on your future career success!*

Exhibit 30.1

Career Impact of a Continuous Learning Regimen

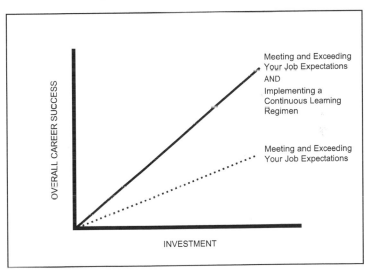

Life is a continuous learning process. Your career, if you really want it to be successful and rewarding, must also follow a continuous learning regimen, and there is no better time to start than right now.

Continuous learning can take many forms. The direction and extent to which you want to pursue it is completely up to you. Your continuous learning regimen should include any activities outside of what you might be exposed to during your normal daily work activities.

Consider a regimen based on small, incremental, and continuous learning and improvement. Small investments of time, with immediate incremental and realized improvements, which can be built upon over time, tend to be the most sustainable and successful.

In Chapter 28 (page 234), we discussed the importance of including personal development activities in your one-year plan. Hopefully you've listed some of those activities you feel would be beneficial. After our review of the many additional options you have, feel free to go back and update your plan.

Start some type of continuous learning regimen, of any kind and no matter how small, and start it now. The success of your career depends on it!

What Is Continuous Learning?

Your options for learning something new are unlimited, constrained only by your imagination, desire, and personal interests. Below are a few of the many options for you to consider:

- Take advantage of employer tuition reimbursement and continuing education programs.

- Research education programs at colleges and universities, including degree, part-time, certificate, and adult learning offerings.

- Inquire about education programs at your local community college.

- Enroll in courses offered at your local park district or community center.

- Visit your local library on a regular basis and take advantage of everything they have to offer: books, research services, librarians and research assistants, educational programs, etc.

- Read career- and industry-related periodicals on a regular basis.

- Read one book (of any kind) every month.

- Read an article-a-week for life. Assuming no one else is doing this, if you read one article each week related to your career or field of study, after a year it will make you fifty-two times more knowledgeable than everyone else you work with.

- Take a class on a topic that is not career-related to broaden your horizons.

- Do you have a passion outside of your career? Pursue it. Start those guitar lessons or take a singing class. Life is too short to wait.

- Sign up for a summer camp this year, as a vacation or as an after-work program.

- Volunteer your time and/or services. *Learn* how to give back.

The Importance of Continuous Learning

- Significantly differentiates you from your competition

- Makes you a more well-rounded individual

- Provides intellectual stimulation, which spurs creative thinking and problem solving skills and abilities

- Helps broaden your scope and depth of knowledge, providing a greater knowledge base to draw from as you chart the future of your career

- Provides topics and material to generate meaningful discussions as you pursue your many relationship development activities

- Provides an additional sense of accomplishment outside of your career

- Prevents you from becoming outdated and stagnant

CHAPTER 31

The First 60 Seconds for Life

And so we come to the end of your journey to learn and understand how to effectively implement *The First 60 Seconds* approach to managing your career. Throughout the book we have focused on, and have reiterated many times, a few themes that provide the basis for *The First 60 Seconds* approach:

- Every person you meet will make a decisive qualification about you within the first 60 seconds of your meeting. Believe it, expect it, and be ready for it.

- Your *First 60 Seconds* encounter can be positively impacted by everything you do prior to that encounter.

- You have only one chance to make a great first impression, then go on and make a great second and third impression as well.

- Focus on differentiation.

- Be proactive in your efforts to effectively manage your career.

Hopefully you have had the opportunity to put many of the strategies into practice and are on your way to implementing a more proactive, closely managed, and successful career plan.

Every Personal Encounter Is a *First 60 Seconds* Encounter

Whether you think about it or not, or whether you want to accept it or not, every encounter you have with another person is a *First 60 Seconds* encounter. Upon meeting someone for the first time and regardless of the situation or circumstances, what transpires in the first 60 seconds of that encounter has a very real and very direct impact on what follows.

Equally important to realize is that you can have many *First 60 Seconds* encounters with the *same person*. Every day, how you greet your spouse in the morning has a direct impact on how you both respond to and treat each other throughout the day. The same holds true for your children, and it especially holds true for your co-workers and the people you meet on a regular basis as you perform your job duties. With people you see on a regular basis, you have the opportunity to make a great first impression every time you see them.

While we talked about having to formally prepare prior to *The First 60 Seconds* encounter at your job interview, for most other career-related and personal encounters, you don't necessarily have to prepare. You just have to remember those important behaviors that we discussed:

- Smile.

- Be happy, confident, excited, and always positive.

- Say, think, and believe, "It is truly a pleasure to meet you!"

- Let people know that you respect their time and that there is no place you would rather be.

- Always have a firm handshake and always make eye contact.

- Strive to develop a relationship; make a connection and make it personal.

That's all there is to it. It's easy to do, takes very little effort, and doing so will continue to differentiate you—in a very positive way—in your career and your life.

 Make the effort and set a goal to maximize all of your *First 60 Seconds* encounters.

The Fine Line between Your Professional and Personal Lives

Why is it important to maximize *all* of your *First 60 Seconds* encounters? The worst case is that you will have done all you can to create a positive experience for you and the person you are with. You might make another great friend. And you never know, you might just make a great impression on a person that could provide your next great career opportunity. You really have nothing to lose.

> The most important reason to maximize all of your *First 60 Seconds* encounters is because the next person you meet with—whether for the first time or not—just might be the person who provides you or leads you to your next great career opportunity.

Our work tends to take up a substantial part of our waking life. Because it is so important in providing for our basic needs and wants, and because we spend so much time and work so hard to be successful in our careers, the line between our personal and work lives can become very blurred. Our personal lives regularly become part of our professional lives, and vice versa.

Consider the following scenarios:

- You run into an old college friend at a restaurant. You haven't seen each other in awhile, but you make the effort to say hello, re-introduce yourself, and make a great first impression as you catch up on lost time. Not only do you rekindle an old friendship, you learn that your friend just so happens to be a high-level manager at the company you always dreamed of working for.

- You're at your child's piano recital and happen to have a few minutes to spare before the performance begins. In the seat next to you is another proud parent. You say hello, introduce yourself, and start up a conversation. The person inquires about your occupation and you give your best ten-second pitch. Interestingly, the person just happens to be the purchasing manager for one of your employer's longest-standing customers, and asks if it would be all right to call you tomorrow to get your ideas on how to take advantage of more of your company's products, which will translate into more sales for you.

- You get a last-minute invitation to go to the company's golf outing this weekend. It happens that the foursome you are placed with includes the vice president of your department's largest internal customer group and she's riding in your cart! You find that she is very approachable and friendly. Not only has she made a great first impression on you, you have made a great first impression on her. During a great round of golf, she takes interest in understanding what you do, and learns that you're the one of the unknown (not any more) heroes in the latest successful project your department has delivered for her.

Every person you meet and speak with on a daily basis, whether in a professional or personal setting, could quite possibly have some positive impact on your career future. If that possibility exists, why not make the effort to make a great first impression *all of the time.*

Baseball is a good example. The more at-bats a player has, the more chances he has to get a hit and thereby increase his batting average. Your at-bats, or personal encounters, are almost limitless, and your ability to get a hit, or effectively manage each personal encounter, is certainly much easier than hitting a 100-mile-per-hour fastball. Step up to the plate, take full advantage of every at-bat you have, and set a goal to continuously increase the number of hits—positive *First 60 Seconds* encounters—that you experience. I think you will find that your career batting average will increase significantly.

 Effectively manage the first 60 seconds of your next job interview and implement *The First 60 Seconds* approach for your life!

The First 60 Seconds
for Life

Whatever your course

Differentiate yourself

Make an impression

Differentiators of *The First 60 Seconds* Approach

🕐 Assess and understand your job and career market.

🕐 Continue to be a champion of the organization while pursuing a new career opportunity.

🕐 Prepare a Company Profile for every company you are interested in.

🕐 Prepare a Job Profile for each and every position you are considering.

🕐 Prepare a Personal Profile of your unique personal qualities.

🕐 Prepare and maintain a Professional Experience Inventory.

🕐 Prepare a comprehensive credentials package, not simply a résumé, to answer all of the questions your prospective employer may have—before they ask them.

🕐 Prepare a Summary of Qualifications for your prospective employer to give them a customized summary of your professional experience, personal attributes, and specifically why you are the best person for the job.

🕐 Provide your prospective employer with a References Summary—before you are asked for it.

🕐 Present your credentials package to a specific person.

🕐 Send a physical copy of your credentials directly to the hiring manager as a way to differentiate yourself from everyone else.

🕐 Do whatever you can to arrange an in-person interview.

🕐 Complete an Interview Scheduling Summary and send a Pre-Interview Letter to the person conducting the interview.

🕐 In all of your interactions, focus on activities that will improve your ability to *share, make known,* and *reveal.*

🕐 Make a concentrated effort to assess and improve your communication skills prior to the interview and *practice, practice, practice.*

🕐 Complete the T-Minus Seven Days Activities for the week prior to your interview.

🕐 Prepare an Interview Agenda.

🕐 Complete the T-Minus One Day Activities.

🕐 Make the effort to improve and perfect your image prior to the interview.

🕐 Complete the Final Preparation Checklist in the thirty minutes prior to your interview.

🕐 Make a positive and lasting *First 60 Seconds* impression.

🕐 Make a personal connection with your interviewer and begin to develop a relationship.

🕐 Effectively utilize your Credentials Package during the interview.

🕐 Address interviewing challenges that may arise—before they arise.

🕐 Use your Personal Profile in the interview to share your nonwork passions and interests, and continue to develop your relationship.

🕐 Effectively use your References Summary during the interview.

🕐 Ask appropriate clarifying and probing questions to solicit and understand what's in it for you.

🕐 Leave the interviewer with the clear understanding that you are interested in the position available, and that there is nothing that would prevent you from accepting the position if offered.

🕐 Prepare a Post-Interview Letter within twenty-four hours of your first interview.

🕐 Send a handwritten Thank-You Letter or Note Card to all interview participants.

- Use the recommended communication options to professionally conclude your job search process with a company you have interviewed with.
- Use the Job Offer Scorecard to evaluate the job offers you are considering.
- Prepare and send an Acceptance of Offer Letter to the company whose offer you are accepting.
- You have one primary objective on your first day of a new job: to effectively manage the first 60 seconds of each encounter with a new person.
- *Bring It On!* Say "yes" when others say "no."
- Commit to continual and incremental career planning and improvement.
- Take into account the rule of compounding interest to manage your long-term compensation growth.
- Implement the ten-for-ten rule into your career planning efforts.
- Continual planning, learning, preparation, differentiation, and taking advantage of every *First 60 Seconds* encounter that may arise will put *you* in complete control of *your* career.
- Develop a written set of career goals and plans.
- Follow and implement the five-step goal setting process.
- Implement a 60 Minutes Per Month Check-Up regimen.
- Implement the six key career growth strategies to effectively prospect for your next career opportunity.
- Start some type of continuous learning regimen, of any kind and no matter how small, and start it now. The success of your career depends on it!
- Make the effort and set a goal to maximize all of your *First 60 Seconds* encounters.
- Effectively manage the first 60 seconds of your next job interview and implement *The First 60 Seconds* approach for your life!

List of Exhibits

1.1 *The First 60 Seconds* Career Management Approach 5

1.2 The 60-Day Plan Timeline 6

1.3 Documentation Process Flow 6

3.1 Company Profile Template 21

4.1 Job Profile Template 26

5.1 Personal Profile Inventory 32

5.2 Personal Profile Example 35

6.1 Professional Experience Inventory 42

7.1 Documentation Process Flow Revisited 45

7.2 Standard Cover Letter 55

7.3 Summary of Qualifications 56

7.4 Sample Résumé Template 57

7.5 References Summary Example 59

8.1 Submission Tracking Template 70

9.1 Interview Scheduling Summary 79

9.2 Pre-Interview Letter Template 80

11.1 Interview Agenda 97

13.1 The First 60 Seconds—Activities and Objectives 108

14.1 Final Preparation Checklist 116

18.1 The First 60 Seconds Completed 141

19.1 Referencing Your Prepared Documentation 150

20.1 Summary of Qualifications Template 158

24.1 Post-Interview Communication Process 189

24.2 The Post-Interview Letter 191

24.3 Secondary Follow-Up Letter 196

24.4 Notice of Offer from Another Company 197

24.5 Acceptance of Offer from Another Company 199

24.6 No Longer Interested in the Position 200

25.1 Employment Agreement Considerations 208

25.2 Job Offer Scorecard 216

25.3 Acceptance of Offer Letter 218

28.1 60-Month Goal Planning Timeline 237

28.2 Needs and Wants Worksheet 240

28.3 Goals Worksheet 242

28.4 One-Year Plan Worksheet 244

30.1 Career Impact of a Continuous Learning Regimen...................... 259

Index

60-Day Plan
  reasons for, 3–4
  summary of, 7
  timeline of, *6*
60-Month Career Plan, 230–232
60-Month Goal, 239, 241

Acceptance of Offer Letter, 217, *218*
Availability, confirming, 179–181

Benefits
  appropriate, 206
  asking about during interview,
    174–175
  in employment agreements,
    211

Career goals
  60-Month Goal, 239, 241
  Goals Worksheet, *242*
  monthly checkup, 243, 245
  need for, 228, 234
  and needs, 237, 238, *240*
  one-year goals, 241
  one-year plan, 243, *244*
  setting, 235–242
  and wants, 238, 239, *240*
Career growth
  and continuous learning, 258
  and mentoring, 254–255
  and modeling successful
    behavior, 256
  and networking, 247–250
  and opportunities outside
    current industry, 253–254
  and opportunities with current
    employer, 8–11, 250–252
  and opportunities within area
    of expertise, 252–253
Career planning
  60-Month Career Plan, 230–232
  as continual process, 227–228
  setting expectations for future,
    228–230
Communication
  assessing skills in, 82–84
  increasing confidence in, 85–88
  key activities of, 82
Companies, researching, 18–22.
  See also Company Profile
Company Profile, 19–20, *21–22*,
  49, 87, 173
Compensation
  appropriate, 206
  negotiating, 210–211
Cover letter, 47–48, *55*
Credentials
  challenges to presentation of,
    62–63
  cover letter, 47–48, *55*
  formatting, 46–47
  and interview preparation, 88

objectives of, 44–45
presenting, objectives of, 61
presenting electronically, 63–65
presenting physically, 63, 66–69
reasons for preparing, 43–44
references, 40, 53–54, *59*,
    168–169
résumé, 50–53, *57–58*, 162–163
reviewing, 91
sending to specific person, 66
Summary of Qualifications,
    48–49, 51, *56*, 157–159
tracking submissions of, 68–70

Documentation Process Flow, 6
Dress, 86, 101, 102–104. *See also*
    Look

Email
    presenting credentials via, 64
    sending post-interview
        communication via,
        192, 193
    use of in job search, 71–72
Employer, current
    being champion of, 11
    opportunities with, 8–11,
        250–252
Employment agreements. *See also*
    Job offers
    benefits in, 211
    components to consider in,
        207–209
    evaluations in, 212
    lack of, 213–214
    need to review, 202
    negotiating compensation in,
        210–211
    non-competition clauses in,
        212–213
Environment, fitting into,
    169–170
Evaluations, performance, 212
Expectations

of interviewer, 150–152
personal, during interview, 153
personal, for future, 228–230
for position, understanding,
    157, 159
Experience
    discussing during interview,
        159–163
    gaps in, 162–163
    and Job Profile, 25
    lack of, 53, 161–162
    Professional Experience
        Inventory, *42*, 49, 51 (*See
        also* Résumé)
    using references to substantiate,
        169

First day, 220, 221

Goals, career. *See* Career goals
Goals Worksheet, *242*
Greeting
    on first day, 221
    during interview, 125–128
    during phone/videoconference
        interview, 140

Human Resources
    and hiring/departmental
        managers, 15
    and opportunities with current
        employer, 10
    role of, 13–14

Information. *See also* Company
    Profile; Job Profile; Personal
    Profile; Professional Experience
    Inventory
    collecting, 7
    Documentation Process Flow, *6*
Interest, confirming, 179–181
Interview
    addressing challenges in, 153–
        154

addressing reasons for leaving
    last job, 163
agenda, 148–149
arranging, 72–77
closing, 181–183
cutting short, 136–137
developing relationship during,
    167–171
discussing experience during,
    159–163
discussing requirements and
    expectations during, 156–
    159
dressing for, 102–104
follow-up communications
    to (See Post-interview
    communications)
formats, 146–148
impact of connection on,
    131–132
importance of doing in person,
    75–76
objectives of, 145–146
pre-interview letter, 77–78, *80*
preparation for (See Interview
    preparation)
providing samples of work
    during, 164–165
questions to ask during,
    173–175
questions to avoid asking
    during, 176–177
satisfying expectations of
    interviewer during,
    150–152
satisfying personal expectations
    during, 153
using Personal Profile during,
    167–168
using Summary of
    Qualifications in, 160
Interview, phone/videoconference,
    74–75, 95–96, 137–140
Interview Agenda, 92, 97, 115, 148

Interview preparation
    day before, 92–93
    four hours before, 93–95
    increasing confidence, 86–88
    need for, 83–84
    practicing for, 87–88, 91
    thirty minutes before, 112–118
    week before, 90–92
Interview Scheduling Summary,
    77, *79*, 91, 115
Introductions, 127, 128

Job, starting, 10, 220, 221
Job offers. *See also* Employment
    agreements
    accepting, 217, 218
    competing, 180–181, 195, *197*,
    198, *199*
    and employee's perspective,
    205–206
    and employer's perspective,
    202–205
    evaluating, 214, 215, *216*
    need to review, 201–202
    questions to ask after receiving,
    214
    time until receiving, 188
Job Offer Scorecard, *216*
Job Profile, 23–25, *26–27*, 49, 61,
    77, 87, 173
Job search. See Career growth;
    Opportunities

Look, 120–124, 139, 221

Managers, hiring/departmental
    delivering credentials to, 67–68
    role of, 14–15
Market forces, 15–16

Needs, 237, 238, *240*
Networking, 247–250
Non-competition clauses, 212–213

One-Year Plan Worksheet, *244*
Opportunities
  within area of expertise, 252–253
  with current employer, 8–11, 250–252
  evaluating, 30
  and *First 60 Seconds* encounters, 264–266
  identifying, 16–17
  and labor and market forces, 15–16
  and networking, 247–250
  outside current industry, 253–254

Personal Profile, 28–34, *35*, 49, 51, 167–168
Personal Profile Inventory, 31, *32*, 52
Planning, career. *See* Career planning
Post-interview communications
  if no longer interested, 198, *200*
  if offered competing position, 195, *197*, 198, 199
  importance of, 187–188
  objectives of, 189
  post-interview letter, 189–192
  secondary follow-up letter, 194–195, *196*
  thank-you note, 192–194
Practice, for interview, 87–88, 91
Pre-interview letter, 77–78, *80*
Professional development, 40
Professional Experience Inventory, 37–41, *42*, 49, 51

Qualifications, summarizing during interview, 150, 156–165. *See also* Qualifications, Summary of
Qualifications, Summary of, 48, 49, 51, *56*, 157–159, 160

Questions
  to ask after receiving job offer, 214
  to ask during interview, 173–175
  non-beneficial, 176–177
  responding to during interview, 150–152

References, 40, 53–54, *59*, 168–169
Relationships
  and career growth, 247–249
  developing, 71, 129–134, 166–171
  developing at new job, 221–222
  importance of, 130, 166
  and Personal Profile, 29–30
  and references, 169
Responsibilities
  for position, understanding, 157
  possibility for growth in, understanding, 174
  in Professional Experience Inventory, 40
Résumé
  gaps in, 162–163
  preparing, 50–53
  sample, *57–58*

Samples of work, 164–165
Self-promotion, importance of, 155. *See also* Qualifications, summarizing during interview
Start time, 180
Submission Tracking Template, *70*
Summary of Qualifications, 48, 49, 51, *56*, 157–159, 160

Thank-you note, 192–194

About the Author

Katie Burns

Dan Burns has realized a successful career as a corporate manager, entrepreneur, educator, business owner, and now as a full-time writer.

For the past fourteen years, Dan has served as owner and executive vice president of a national technical and management consulting company, providing consulting and employee placement services to *Fortune* 500 companies and helping people successfully obtain their next great career opportunity.

Dan was born and raised in Chicago, and currently resides with his family in La Grange, Illinois.

Comments and inquiries can be sent to Dan directly at: dan@ thefirstsixtyseconds.com

 Please visit *The First 60 Seconds* website for additional information and resources: www.thefirstsixtyseconds.com